Transformed:
My Story as a Farmer's Daughter with Big Dreams & an Even Bigger God

Allison R. Smith

DEDICATION

For my daughters, Avery and Natalie.
You girls can do anything as long as you have the courage to try.

CONTENTS

ACKNOWLEDGMENTS

First and foremost, I have to thank God for putting this book in my heart and giving me the courage to write it. You have shown me value in every season and every experience in my life, transforming me along the way.

Thank you to my parents for planting the seed in my faith journey, guiding me and encouraging me to love God and love others. Thank you for instilling in me a strong work ethic, a kind heart, and a desire to serve.

Many thanks to my Grandparents for growing my faith, loving me and supporting me as I grew into the person I am today. You were the first story tellers, and I wish you were here to read mine.

I am grateful for my friends, my mentors, and people who have inspired me over the years to do hard things, step into my fears, and grow as a person. Thank you for helping me to realize my full potential and for providing support and encouragement along the way.

Thank you, Pastor Gary for encouraging me to not leave this Earth before sharing my testimony and my story. Thank you for always speaking truth and teaching us how to not only live well but die well. I will never forget you and the impact you had on my life.

To my husband, Ted. Thank you for loving me well and always supporting my dreams. You have often been the one to go ahead, paving the way for me to see that I can also do hard things. Thank you for challenging me to push past my fears and insecurities, work hard, but also take time to play hard. I love you and the beautiful life we have created together.

Endless thanks to my girls, Avery and Natalie, for inspiring me to know better, do better, and be better. This book is for you. I started this writing process just wanting to tell you my story, and somewhere along the way I felt inspired to write an entire book. God put it in my heart to share every chapter of my story, even the chapters that were difficult. Thank you for cheering me on along the way. Thank you for all the hugs and encouraging words. I love you, and I love being your Mom.

INTRODUCTION

"Seasons change and so do we." Unknown

Everyone has a story, and purpose and lessons can be found in every chapter of our story if we have the courage to share it. Stories have been a part of my life since I was a little girl. Whether it was reading someone else's story or writing my own, the written word has always been powerful for me. Over the years, writing has allowed me to express myself without having to speak the words out loud. Like many people, public speaking is one of my worst fears that I continue to battle today. The written word has always come easier for me, giving me a voice in a world filled with noise. Our words have value, and our stories are important. Our experiences mold us into the person we are meant to be, and when shared can encourage and inspire others as well. As I've gotten older, reflecting back on my roots as a simple country girl, acknowledging all the fears, self-doubt, and failures I've had to overcome while pursing my dreams, I felt God tugging on my heart to share my story. We all fight our own battles, big and small, experience failures, and go through tough seasons that make us stronger as a result. This is my story, my personal growth journey to a more fulfilling life, and all the lessons I've learned along the bumpy path. If nothing else, this is a gift for my girls, a bit of a memoir filled with encouragement and a hefty dose of Jesus.

I grew up as a farmer's daughter surrounded by corn fields and pastures, modest houses, and hard-working people. I was blessed with loving parents, a stable home, and had opportunities for unique experiences as a country girl. But instead of savoring my innocent childhood and appreciating the life I had, I often wished to escape my small town and simple country upbringing, anxious to grow up and enter the next season of my life. Despite my accomplishments early in life, I was often unfulfilled and couldn't wait to leave and pursue something bigger and better. I wanted to be a nurse, marry a doctor, and live in a big city filled with excitement and opportunity. I dreamed of a life with a couple of kids, nice friends, travel, and fun adventures. I wanted change. As a dreamer and a goal-getter, I wanted more for my life. But what I failed to see is that my life on the farm was actually a pretty amazing gift. Growing up in the country taught me invaluable lessons about hard work, family, and faith. I just didn't see the unique value of my time in the country until many years later. My teenage years were filled with busyness and achievements, but also feelings of loneliness, anxiety, confusion, and self-doubt. The opinions of others weighed heavily on my heart and often made me question who I was and what was most important in life. Despite being incredibly self-driven to do well and accomplish big things, I struggled with confidence, self-worth, and feeling joy. I constantly felt an internal battle between wanting to work hard and achieve big dreams versus wanting to run and hide and play small instead of standing out. I definitely had a lot of growing to do, and thankfully God continued to pursue me and slowly transform me into the more confident, fulfilled and joyful person I am today. It's been quite a journey, and I am who I am because of my experiences and the transformation that finally occurred.

Just as farming involves seasons of cultivating, sowing, fertilizing, and harvest; life is also full of similar seasons, and sometimes certain seasons are hard. We stumble, we fall, we learn, we change, and we try to move on and grow from our experiences. God shows us unbelievable beauty and invaluable growth in every season if we choose to see it. Our heaviest seasons, no matter how big or small, transform us and can provide light to others if we decide to share them. My desire to create a book that not only serves as a memoir for my daughters, but also inspires them as well as others to have faith, dream big and grow with an even bigger God is how this book came to fruition. In the chapters ahead, I will share stories from my childhood in the country to becoming a wife and working mom and everything in between. I will share my most vulnerable stories of dealing with anxiety, overcoming fears and failures to becoming a happier, more fulfilled version of myself. This is my story of personal growth and transformation as I've walked through many seasons of life. I have learned that God is bigger and better than any dream I ever had, any insecurity, fear or failure I had to overcome, and I hope you discover that in your own story as well. Let's begin, shall we?

Allison R. Smith

CHAPTER 1:

MY EARLY CHILDHOOD

*"One of the luckiest things that can happen to you in
life is to have a happy childhood and a loving home."*
Agatha Christie

I feel like I should start from the very beginning and paint the picture
of my childhood, my move to the country and everything that
followed in order to show you my personal growth journey. This
first chapter might take you on a bit of a ride down memory lane as I
reflect on what is was like to grow up in the 80's. It was simple and
sweet. The 90's were a different story, but only because I was a
teenager during those years. You'll hear more about that later.

My story began in a small rural Texas community as I made my
exciting entrance into the world on a cold January night in 1980. I
was a difficult birth, born breach during natural labor, and my Dad
wasn't even allowed to be in the delivery room. Who ever thought
that was a good idea? Despite my challenging entry into the world,
my parents were thrilled to have a little girl, and gave me the name
Allison Renee. At the time, I had an older brother, Justin, and less
than 2 years later; we were joined by our younger brother, Brad, and
our family was complete. I grew up as the middle child, the only girl,

sandwiched between 2 boys who often butted heads, as siblings like to do. My first two years as a baby were spent in my parent's first home, a little white farmhouse out in the country. They'd only been married a few years when I was born as they created quite the instant family. We quickly outgrew the space, as Brad came along, and ended up moving to a bigger house in town. This is the house that I remember from my early childhood. It was a simple 3-bedroom, 2 bath peach brick home around the block from our elementary school. My Dad was a self-employed farmer, just like his Dad and Grandpa, and my Mom stayed at home with us kids before eventually returning to work as the school nurse in our town. My Dad's farming business was steadily growing as my parents raised us kids in the perfect little neighborhood. It was truly small town, America. The streets were safe, the neighbors were kind, there were friends to play with, and we were only a mile away from our church which was great.

I have simple, but also unique memories of growing up in town. Having a farmer for a Dad, a giant tractor tire appropriately served as our sandbox. We'd often climb trees or play in our two-story wooden playhouse, just using our imaginations. My Dad and an uncle built that playhouse, and it definitely got lots of use as we'd play "house." I remember cooling off in the summers with the slipping slide or little plastic pool in our backyard, enjoying my Mom's concoction of "ground up Kool-Aid," basically a homemade version of a Sonic slush. We thought they were the best thing ever. Grape was always my favorite. I also have sweet memories of us sitting in the front yard waiting on the ice-cream truck to come down our street. That familiar song could be heard playing several blocks away, as we'd run inside to grab money for our favorite cold treat. My parents would often take us on long bike rides around town. I remember always having skinned up knees from falling off my bike when we came to a stop sign. That was back before helmets and all the other safety measures that now exist, but we all somehow survived, right?

The scariest incident with me occurred when I was maybe 6 or 7 years old. I remember sitting on the back of my Dad's grain trailer that was parked in front of our house, suddenly losing my balance and landing on the pavement, my head taking the brunt of the fall. It was quite scary as I was knocked unconscious and had to be rushed to the local doctor's office. I remember being confused and sick to my stomach, and I threw up all over the exam room. If memory serves me well, it was red, and it was everywhere. I had a big bump on my forehead and apparently suffered a pretty bad concussion. I felt that bump on my head for years. I was lucky as my injury could have been much worse.

By that time, my parents had already walked through several frightening experiences with us kids. Justin came down with whooping cough as a baby and nearly died. My parents were given little hope, and were told to bring in the pastor, but somehow, he pulled through. He was quite the miracle baby. Brad broke his leg going down a slide when he was not even 2. He had to be in traction and then in a body cast for weeks. That was the first of many broken bones for Brad, and definitely not his worst accident. You'll hear more about that later.

Life in the 80's was quite simple, as everything seemed to move at a much slower pace, and I viewed the world through my rose-colored lenses. My early childhood was filled with happy little memories split between our house in town and the fields my Dad farmed. If there was stress, I didn't see it. If there was tension, I didn't feel it. My parents provided a fun, loving home for us kids as my Dad worked hard to grow his farming business. We grew up on classic country music, like George Strait, singing "Amarillo by Morning" in the back of our suburban. I played with Barbies and Cabbage Patch Dolls, later collecting Garbage Pail Kids trading cards. My brothers were into baseball cards like most boys their age. Weekends were often spent skating at the old green skating rink just outside of town. Besides the local swimming pool, it was basically the only thing to do.

I can still recall the dusty birthday plates tacked up on the walls and when I hear a Michael Jackson song these days, such as "Thriller," it takes me back to skating round and round that old skating rink. We all became great skaters from a young age, holding onto my Dad's belt from behind until we were able to do it on our own. I think everyone had at least a few of their birthday parties there. It was definitely the place to be.

Our favorite restaurant was one of the only restaurants in town. Oh, how we looked forward to those steak finger baskets and ice-cream blizzards at the local Dairy Queen. Eating out was quite the luxury back then, and we didn't do it very often. Meals were simple and often eaten at home. Movies were also simple, but a huge part of my childhood. We grew up watching The Goonies, ET and Back to Future. My personal favorite was the Parent Trap, starring Hayley Mills from Pollyanna. I'm sure I wore out that VHS tape, watching it at least a hundred times. It's funny thinking about having to rewind tapes before watching them again. Oh, how times have changed.

Communication was also quite different back then as we talked on house phones with cords that stretched for miles. You remember that, right? Cell phones and the internet didn't exist until many years later. Communicating with people required a phone call to their house and searching for information required looking through piles and piles of books. I think every house at that time had a set of encyclopedias on a bookshelf, along with a dictionary and a medical reference book of some sort. Like I said, it was simpler times and slower days. There were no computers or electronic devices to play on. No google search, no social media, no Amazon Prime, and definitely no Siri or Alexa. How did we ever survive? Even cameras were not digital. Taking film to be developed was always a gamble, as sometimes the entire roll of film was a complete wash. I remember how excited we were when the Nintendo Entertainment System came out. It was our first introduction to video games and we absolutely loved Super Mario Brothers. Video games have definitely come a long way since then, but some games never get old.

Just like everything else, our family vacations were also quite modest and usually involved going to a Texas water park or amusement park. Since our lives revolved around planting and harvest and we were living off of one income at the time, it didn't really afford us much time or budget for travel. We didn't leave the state of Texas until I was in junior high, and that was probably the case for a lot of my friends growing up.

As much as we loved our house and the convenience of living in town, my Dad's farming business was growing and evolving, and it eventually made sense for us to move to the country where his land and equipment was. My early childhood in town taught me about the simple joys of childhood, being kind to our neighbors, and using my imagination. We spent almost all of our free time outside, just playing and exploring with friends and being kids. It was a care-free time in my life with great memories. Moving to the country changed everything, but also taught me the most about life and what's truly important.

Allison R. Smith

CHAPTER 2:

MY LIFE AS A COUNTRY GIRL

"You can take the girl out of the country, but you can't take the country out of the girl." Unknown

The second half of my childhood was spent living in the country. We traded blacktop and neighborhood friends for dirt roads and corn fields. My parents purchased an older house on 100 acres of land with a creek that also included a barn and a shop to store farm equipment. There was a big driveway for playing basketball and a little storage shed that us kids quickly claimed as our "playhouse." The house was remodeled right way, since 70's shag carpet and green appliances weren't really our thing, and eventually 2 more bedrooms and an additional bathroom were added on to give us kids more space. We were about 5 miles out of town and lived off a half mile dirt road that we would later loathe as we grew older and had cars of our own. We would literally drive 5 miles an hour down the road only to be met by an oncoming truck that immediately kicked up dust all over our freshly washed car. Keeping our cars sparkling clean was a lost cause, but we sure did try.

Living in the country was incredibly peaceful, filled with pretty sunsets, cool breezes, and fields of green. However, it also felt isolated, like we were miles away from everything, stuck in the middle of nowhere. As an adolescent who missed her friends, I remember being quite upset with my parents for moving us out there. Being in the country was not only lonely, but it scared me. I'd often make my Mom lay in bed with me at night and I'd cry if she tried to leave. I was always worried that someone or some scary thing was going to get me. It was dark and there were weird sounds and I worried that every car coming down our dirt road was a bad guy. I was also deathly afraid of snakes and all sorts of other country critters. The boys enjoyed it way more than I did. They loved riding the 4-wheeler, fishing at the tank, playing in the creek, and having campfires. It was one giant playground for them. Unfortunately, a 4-wheeler incident in the creek with my Mom kept me from ever driving it again. I still remember us flipping over, worried about the hot engine burning our legs, my Mom trying to push it off of us, and for some reason I think I got stung by ants in the water. It was a frightening experience that I never wanted to live through again. I was definitely a scaredy-cat when it came to lots of things, especially the creek, steep hills and uneven ground, and I still am today. As far as I'm concerned, the creek is full of snakes and if I drive up a hill or on the side of a cliff, the car will most certainly tip over and I will be dead. Therefore, I'm not a fan of creeks or parking on any type of incline. I try to avoid it at all costs. I also avoid parallel parking and most automatic car washes, but that's a different story.

Our trampoline was one of our most memorable Christmas gifts after moving out to the country. My parents had arranged for the trampoline to be delivered and assembled on Christmas Eve night. It was our big gift, and they stayed up late that night nervous that our house wouldn't be found in the dark, and the trampoline wouldn't be there in the morning. They eventually went to sleep at about 4am, and they were just as surprised as we were when we ran outside on Christmas morning and saw our gift from Santa sitting there in the yard. It was the Christmas miracle we would talk about for years. It provided all sorts of entertainment for us kids, and maybe resulted in a few injuries as well. This was way before protective pads and nets existed. We enjoyed laying on the trampoline at night, as it gave us the best view of the stars in the sky, another perk to living out in the country.

My Dad also built a backstop for the boys to hit baseballs, as well as a volleyball court and a tree house. We'd often invite friends to come out and play. They thought it was great, especially all of Brad's friends. Country living gave us plenty of room to explore and use our imaginations. We could make all the noise we wanted and hit all the baseballs and golf balls without fear of hitting anyone else's windows. Unfortunately, our windows were still at risk. I remember playing in bales of hay out in the barn, turning it into a big playhouse, jumping from bale to bale, probably making a huge mess. I can't believe my parents let us do that, or maybe they didn't know. Were we not even worried about snakes? You know I hated snakes and still do today. A snake is a snake, and I wouldn't be caught dead in a barn full of hay at this point in my life.

You're not really living in the country unless you have animals, and we had more dogs and cats and kittens than I can recall. Most of them just sort of showed up, probably dumped by others, and made themselves at home. Unfortunately, living out in the country also meant that most animals weren't around long. They wondered off, had to be taken away due to bothering the neighbor's chickens or cattle, they got run over by trucks, got into the engines of cars or became poisoned by chemicals around the shop. I loved having animals, as they always brought so much comfort, but it was also pretty traumatic when they died. Country life was hard on animals. We briefly had a horse named Buttercup, but we just didn't have enough time to devote to her, as horses require a tremendous amount of work. Cattle briefly roamed our pastures, but my Dad decided that farming was his passion, and raising cattle not so much. My brothers raised pigs when they were in high school and earned good money at the local shows. I never got into it as I had too many other activities, but I sure did learn a lot by watching my brothers participate.

Growing up in the country, we all learned to drive well before our 16th birthday, one of the many perks of being a country kid. The boys were driving tractors as soon as their feet could touch the clutch, and I learned to drive my parent's cars on dirt roads, often driving my Mom around from field to field. One time I made the mistake of pushing the gas pedal instead of the break, causing my Mom and me to go flying into the ditch. Don't you know I never made that mistake again? When I was 15, I got my hardship license so I could drive back and forth to school and activities. My Dad bought me a dependable red 2-door cavalier off a used car lot in town. I loved having my own car, as it gave me a little bit of freedom. I no longer felt so isolated in the country, as I could just drive into town when I wanted to. On the weekends, we would often drive around the big loop in town, also known as "the drag." We thought we were pretty cool, as we played music with the windows rolled down, stopping to chat with friends. Fortunately, this was when gas was super cheap. I wonder if the kids today still do that for fun. I would say, probably not since the introduction of smart phones, social media, and everything else that kids are entertained with these days.

When I graduated with the incredible honor as Valedictorian of my class earning college scholarships, my Dad decided to upgrade my car to a new white sporty Cavalier as I headed off to college. He loved taking care of me when it came to my car. He was always keeping an eye on the tires, gas, and oil changes. He knew how to fix anything and everything. He was definitely the first person I would call if I had a problem with my car, and I know I can still call him today. Too bad I didn't actually learn how to change a tire or check my own oil like any respectable country girl, but my Dad felt like a girl shouldn't have to do those things, or maybe I never showed any interest in learning. Either way, I appreciate him always looking after me.

Farming was a way of life for our family. Part of the year was spent preparing the land and sowing the seeds, and summers were spent harvesting the wheat, milo and corn. As a farmer's daughter, I was surrounded by tall corn fields, John Deere tractors, and giant silos for storing grain. My life felt like the country music song, "John Deere Green." The hot summer days and nights were often spent riding in the tractor or combine with my Dad or my brothers. We'd pack a cooler of drinks and snacks and chat while listening to music together, watching the fruits of my Dad's labor come in. I remember one summer riding in the grain cart with Justin, getting so excited when our favorite song "Toy Soldiers" came on the radio. When you ride in the tractor long enough, you hear the same songs over and over again. You can almost predict when certain songs will come on. That was one song we looked forward to hearing, and we'd crank it up nice and loud, "Step by step, heart to heart, left right left, we all fall down… like toy soldiers." There's so much truth in those lyrics as we all go through life falling down and learning to get back up again. I bet I was thinking that as I sang those words nice and loud in the tractor with my big brother, right? Or maybe I just liked the popular pop song of the 90's. Either way, those were great memories.

Picnic time was also treasured time during the season of harvest. We enjoyed eating countless picnics in the field that often consisted of fried chicken, mashed potatoes, and baked beans or some variation of that. It was traditional southern cooking, and my Mom was a great cook. We often had homemade desserts such as cobbler or banana pudding. There was always iced tea, and even a jug of water to wash dirty hands with. My Mom took thoughtful care to make sure everyone had what they needed to eat and then get right back to work. Sandwiches just wouldn't do. She felt like those hard-working guys needed a hearty homemade meal to refuel them for the hot afternoon. Those meals were cherished time together, as harvest involved long hours in the field. It was hot and dusty and lots of work. It was definitely a family affair.

Our life revolved around planting and harvest seasons. For my Dad, the days often started before the sun came up and ended late at night depending on what was going on. I grew up knowing more about the weather than most kids, as farming is hugely dependent on it. For instance, a few inches of rain at just the right time could mean the difference between a good crop and a bad crop. One tiny freeze could mean replanting entire fields. We now own a rain gage so when my parents ask how much rain we got; we can proudly tell them 2 tenths of an inch. I also learned all about things like rotating crops, fertilizing, grain storage, and sunflowers. To a farmer, all sunflowers are bad, despite their beauty in the sunlight. I don't think I ever had to chop sunflowers, but my Dad undoubtedly chopped his fair share. And he certainly didn't bring them home to be placed in a pretty vase.

As I grew older, I learned to help my Mom prepare these elaborate meals, take them to the field, and then go home and clean up the kitchen, and start the entire process again for supper. If the guys were combining near the house, we would enjoy meals around the table. There were often hired hands that joined us and felt like family. They were usually high school or college guys that wanted a summer job. Those summers working for my Dad probably taught them all sort of invaluable lessons about hard work and family values. Besides assisting in the kitchen, I also helped around the house, cleaning and doing laundry. There were always piles and piles of laundry with a family of 5, including 3 guys with stinky dirty clothes from the field. Our washer and dryer ran daily. I also washed cars by hand and helped with outside chores and eventually learned to use the riding lawn mower. When you live out in the country, mowing the lawn can be an all-day chore, but also an opportunity to work on your summer tan. That part I liked. There was always something to do, endless chores to be done, and I learned how to do them. I always kept busy, always looked for things that needed to be cleaned or organized, and even today, I'm not much for sitting around.

My brothers learned from an early age how to drive the tractors and helped with harvest during our summer break from school. It became their summer job, and they looked forward to it every year. Or maybe it was the money they looked forward to. Either way, my Dad would pay them for their hours of hard work, and I soon wanted to earn my own money as well. One summer, I decided I could drive that grain cart if they could, and I gave it my best shot. After all, I had learned to drive the riding lawn mower. I quickly realized that it was much harder than it looked. It made me nervous, trying to keep up with the combine and then unload it into the truck without spilling corn everywhere. Corn on the ground was basically like dollar bills thrown into the trashcan. After a few tries, I decided I was best used in the kitchen or doing housework. My parents started paying me for doing my part around the house, as that work was just as important as the work that was being done in the fields.

Eager to have a "real job," I eventually went to work at a cute little gift shop in town, called the Busy Bee. Our neighbor along with her sister owned and operated the shop, and I worked there for a summer, perfecting my gift-wrapping skills. I also learned how to count back money from a cash register and how to provide customer service. I can still remember the smells of that gift and floral shop, and I can still hear the bell clanging as people came through the front door. It was a good first job at the age of 15, and I appreciated the opportunity. Later on, after turning 16, I got a job at H-E-B grocery store, initially as a bagger, quickly moving up to cashier. It felt like a real job with real paychecks, and I enjoyed the independence that it gave me. I held that job through the rest of high school and even into my first year or two of college. I liked working and found immense value in working from an early age. I saw that there is purpose in all types of work, and I learned how to save and manage my own money. This work ethic would carry over into my career as a nurse and then a nurse practitioner in the years to come.

It was during my years as a country girl that I really learned how to work hard and maintain a home. I learned by watching, as my parents both modeled an incredible work ethic to us kids. I watched my Dad start with something small and slowly grow it into a large successful farming operation, all while remaining incredibly honest and humble. I watched my Mom work alongside him, supporting him as a good farmer's wife while also working at her own job as the school nurse. My parents taught us that you have to work hard for what you have, that nothing comes free, and us 3 kids definitely learned and understood that lesson from a young age. I knew that I wouldn't be a 4th generation farmer like my brothers were learning to be, but I looked forward to becoming a good wife and a working mom and having a house of my own someday.

I dreamed of becoming a nurse in the hospital, using my big heart to care for others in their time of need. I knew I wanted to be a nurse from a young age and also envisioned myself working while raising a family. Working hard and serving people was in my DNA and felt like my calling from God. Those years of watching, learning and growing on the farm provided the foundation for my strong work ethic I have today. I saw my parents wake up early, work hard for their family, while still making time for us kids. It's why I now wake up before the sun to fry eggs and bacon for my own family before work and school. It's why I pride myself in keeping a clean welcoming home for us to enjoy. It's why despite working outside the home, I still take the time to fry chicken and make mashed potatoes for my girls, because there's nothing like home-cooked meals, and they love it. It's why we plant a garden every year and show our girls where food comes from. They love running out to check all the plants and pick the biggest tomatoes and squash and other veggies. They love cooking and baking in the kitchen with us. Our girls will leave home knowing how to maintain a home and cook for their families, because we have shown them how to do so.

Those years living out in the country gave me a unique appreciation for all of life's little blessings like beautiful sunrises and stunning sunsets, the sound of the wind blowing, the smell of the rain coming in, green pastures and wheat fields, flowing creeks, the sound of frogs, and the taste of fresh vegetables. It's why I won't run anywhere but outside in nature, so I can look around and appreciate God's beautiful creation. On one of my recent runs, I spotted an ear of corn lying in someone's yard. Only a farmer's daughter would notice an ear of corn in a neighborhood far from the cornfields. I picked it up, inspecting the size of the kernels, and I was instantly taken back to my childhood on the farm. As much as I loved the convenience of living in town when I was a kid and often tried so hard to escape the farm life, I learned that there is nothing like growing up in the country, and I am eternally grateful for my childhood experience.

Valuable Lessons I learned while growing up a farmer's daughter:

1. Work hard and get down and dirty if you need to. Farming is not an 8-5 office job that you get dressed up for and come home and rest from. Farming is long days and endless work. It's waking up before the sun and working often past dark, sometimes pulling all-nighters if rain is on the way. I watched my Dad spend exhausting hours preparing the land, sowing the seeds, fertilizing and praying over the young plants, only to watch a bad storm destroy hundreds of acres. I watched him completely replant crops after a late freeze. I watched him get down and dirty fixing equipment and cleaning out grain bins, always coming home with dirty, bruised, cut up hands. You'll never meet a farmer with soft, clean hands, but instead callused arthritic hands of someone that works hard. I too grew up not afraid of getting my hands dirty, making mud pies in the backyard as kids, walking bare foot down the

gravel road, playing in creeks and hay bales. I also learned to work from an early age, whether it was helping out with cooking or chores around the house, or eventually getting a job of my own. I learned valuable life skills out on the farm that prepared me for life as an adult.

2. Plan ahead. With farming, there are good years and bad years, and you have to prepare for both. So much of the business is dependent on the weather as well as the price in the market. You can work just as hard as the year before, but lack of rain or too much rain or low market value can really affect the profit you bring in. My parents learned to save and prepare for those tough years. I too learned to save, as we all had savings accounts from a very young age. My parents taught us how to plan for the future and manage our money wisely.

3. Take a leap of faith. Farming is definitely a business that requires an incredible amount of faith over fear. Each year is different, often with unpredicted challenges. You have to be comfortable taking risks even when you are not sure it will be successful. Bad weather, broken down equipment, fuel prices, market prices are just some of the challenges that can affect having a successful year. But as a farmer, you continue to persevere, taking that leap of faith year after year.

4. Count your blessings. When your job is so dependent on the weather, you learn to be thankful for every drop of rain in the middle of a drought, grateful for every sunny day during a wet season, and to give thanks for all things from up above. Our prayers growing up always included thanking God for the rain or praying to God for more rain or more sunshine for the crops. We thanked Him for our health and ability to work and serve others. We looked at each day as a blessing and an opportunity. Even today, I still thank God when we get rain or see a pretty rainbow across the sky, reminding us of His promise. We count our blessings, big and small. These

simple prayers growing up showed me that no prayer request is too small, and we should certainly give thanks for even the smallest blessings such as an inch of rain.

5. Family is important. Farming is definitely a family business. A family that works together stays together. All hands were needed and appreciated during summer harvest. Whether it was combining the field, transferring the grain from the grain cart to the truck, hauling the grain off to be sold or stored, moving equipment from one field to another, refueling vehicles, fixing equipment, preparing meals for the workers, packing coolers, washing laundry, or one of the other endless tasks around the farm, it took help from everyone. Summers were spent working, but there was also a huge focus on family. Those meals in the field, that time in the combine, dinners around the table, bedtime prayers for rain were all about our time as a family. My parents made sure we knew that family was important.

6. Learn to respect. Watching my Grandpa and my Dad show respect for land conservation, the crops they produced, and the people they did business with showed me that God's creation and His people deserve respect. All people, young or old, our animals, one's land and property, as well as the country we live in and the flag we fly deserves our respect. My parents always encouraged us to be kind, work hard, and be respectful members of society.

7. Be creative. Growing up in the country fostered my creativity. Living in the middle of nowhere (actually only 5 miles from town) forced me to use my imagination, play independently, and find ways to grow. We didn't have electronic devices or cell phones, nor did we have neighborhood friends to play with. To avoid boredom, I would often read books and write letters, create things, and explore. I became quite the independent person, happily content with doing things on my own, and finding pleasure in

the simplest things like watching an old movie or listening to music and organizing my room. I am still that way today.

8. Enjoy the little moments in life. Living on a farm gave me some unique childhood memories that not everyone gets to grow up with. I had a giant playground as my backyard that afforded me adventures and a creative imagination. I learned to drive from a young age, I rode in tractors and combines, caught fish and skipped rocks across the creek, ate meals in the middle of a corn field, rode around in the back of a truck bed, drank water straight from the hose, cracked and shelled pecans and snapped black eyed peas until my fingers were sore, and gazed at the starry sky while enjoying the peace and quiet you only can experience out in the country. These little moments didn't feel so glorious when I was a teenager but looking back on all of them now makes me smile. What a gift it was to grow up in the country. I am now so much more appreciative of little things in life, and I try to create some of the same meaningful memories with my girls.

I grew up as a farmer's daughter with country roots, always dreaming of something bigger and better, not realizing what a blessing it was. I don't think I realized the full impact it had on me and my life until I had a family of my own. I now see the incredible value that season had in my life. These valuable lessons I learned during my time in the country provided the foundation for the life I live today, and I am now grateful for my childhood in the country.

Most of us are not lucky enough to grow up in the country, nor are we raising our kids in the country, but some of these same lessons can be taught and learned exactly where we are. We can bring a piece of the country to our own back yard by planting a garden and watching the little plants grow. We can cook and bake with our kids showing them how to make homemade meals to enjoy around the table. We can raise animals, care for pets, and sometimes even have egg laying chickens if the city allows it. We can shop at local farmer's markets, pick up pecans at the park, and have family picnics. We can take our kids fishing and camp under the stars. We can teach the value of hard work by doing yard work together, washing cars in the driveway with a bucket of soapy water, and doing chores around the house. We can foster creativity by going on hikes, exploring new places, or building things out of reusable resources. My girls can a take a giant Amazon box and some hot glue guns and turn that box into a Barbie house in a matter of hours. Kids need unique opportunities to learn and grow. Each day is a priceless gift, every day and every season has purpose, and we must not take for granted the time we have on this Earth.

"To everything there is a season, and a time to every purpose under the heaven: A time to be born, a time to die; a time to plant, and a time to pluck up that which is planted; A time to kill, and a time to heal; a time to break down, and a time to build up; A time to weep, and a time to laugh; a time to mourn, and a time to dance." Ecclesiastes 3: 1-4 (NIV)

Allison R. Smith

CHAPTER 3:

CHEERS TO THE TEENAGE YEARS

"In order to love who you are, you cannot hate the experiences that have shaped you." Andrea Dykstra

I'm not sure if my teenage years were more challenging for me or for my parents. Either way, I'm glad I was only a teenager once, because once was enough, right? From the outside, it probably looked like I had it all together, as I did all the things, worked hard and applied myself, and actually ended up as Valedictorian of my high school class. I was ambitious and self-driven, goal minded and achievement oriented. I said yes to everything that was asked of me, probably saying yes to too many things if I'm honest with you. I was independent and maybe even a little bit strong-willed if you ask my parents. I had big dreams and high expectations for my future self, but I also had a big heart, and that heart was often hurting inside. I was fighting my own battles with anxiety, insecurity, and feelings of confusion as I entered high school, and it only got worse from there. Certain people and situations led me down a road of self-doubt. Opinions of others weighed heavily on my ability to feel confident. I almost felt like I needed to play smaller in order to just blend in and not stand out, and sometimes I made choices that definitely did that.

In a way, my joy felt stolen, as I almost felt like I couldn't celebrate my achievements. I started questioning my ambition and self-worth. I wondered if what I was doing was worth the teasing and negative comments I sometimes received. Not everyone treated me that way, but the few who did made those years difficult for me. I just wanted to work hard and do well. I wasn't looking for applause, just kindness and acceptance for who I was. It was a confusing time in my life, as it probably is for most teenagers. And I can only imagine what it's like today with all the technology and social media that now exists.

Our small town had about 4500 people. It literally felt like we knew everyone and everything. I had 70 kids in my class growing up, and a lot of us spent Kindergarten through 12th grade together. That was both a good thing and maybe a bad thing, as a lot of us probably grew tired of each other. I was friends with the same group of about 20 girls off and on throughout my entire childhood. They were girls I not only went to school with, but spent time with at church and all the other various activities we participated in. We played sports together, had sleepovers together, cheered together, and played in the band with one another. Some of us even worked together.

Unfortunately, several of my closest friends moved away in our late junior high years, a huge reason for my anxiety as I entered high school. These friends brought me joy and made me want to level up. They were smart and also ambitious, but also just fun to be around. It was an overwhelmingly sad season, as I said tearful goodbyes to one good friend after another. Tara was the friend whose move hurt the most. Some of my most fun years were with my junior high BFF, Tara. She was a girl that lit up the room simply with her presence. Her smile and laughter were contagious, and I couldn't get enough of her. At times, we were inseparable. We were so much alike and spent almost all of our time together since we participated in all the same activities. Tara also lived out in the country, but on the other side of town. Lots of our time was spent having sleepovers, exploring and doing things that country kids do. I adored her fun family and was absolutely devastated when they had to move.

In junior high, Tara and I were both obsessed with the 90's boy band New Kids on the Block. Wasn't every teenage girl back then? I actually got to meet 2 members of NKOTB on a family trip to Disney World. It was our first time on an airplane, and we spotted them on our way back. That's right, I have a picture with Joey McIntyre in his early years, and I am wearing a silly Daisy Duck hat and all! I proudly displayed a poster size print of it on my wall for years, along with other fan gear. One of me and Tara's favorite things to do was make our own mixed cassette tapes with my little boom box. We would piece together songs from NKOTB and others such as Garth Brook's "Friends in low places" with UB40's "Red, Red Wine" and add in our own voices to create the perfect mix. We spent hours doing this as I'm sure a lot of 90's kids did. Tara was a really special friend, like a sister, and it broke my heart into a million pieces when she announced that she would be moving to Mississippi near the end of our 7th grade year. I remember saying goodbye to her after a track meet one night and crying the entire way home.

Life as I knew it would never be the same, especially after a couple more of my close friends moved away in the following years. It was probably the most difficult season of my childhood, as the happier, more adventurous, confident version of me was replaced with a more anxious, insecure version. Tara had brought out the best in me (and a lot of people), and for some reason when she left, that fun confident version of myself also left. It was like a piece of my heart went with her to Mississippi when we said goodbye, and it took years and years to get it back. We wrote letters back and forth for years, promising to always stay friends and eventually reunite, but we never saw each other again. It was difficult getting through 8th grade followed by the high school years without Tara. I thought of her often, even as we both got busy and eventually stopped writing. The dynamics of my group of friends started to change in high school, and nothing really felt the same after Tara left.

In a small school like ours, the same kids participated in literally everything, and I was most certainly one of those kids. My long list of extra-curricular activities helped mold me into an incredibly well-rounded student with great balancing skills when I graduated, but also resulted in me feeling a little burned out. I loved being busy but taking on too many things resulted in me not having enough time to dedicate myself to the areas where I was gifted. I was good at a lot of things, but not really great at any one thing. I stretched myself pretty thin, saying yes to almost everything including band, cheerleading, sports, and UIL amongst other things.

Band was probably one of my most favorite activities. I played the flute all through school, even marching in the band with my cheerleader uniform on during half time shows. Only in a small town is that possible. Our little band was quite good, even going to state one year. My friend Kristen and I went back and forth between 1st and 2nd chair all through school, always sitting next to each other. I also played the piano for many years and ended up playing Pomp and Circumstance for Graduation when I was a freshman and my older brother was a senior. Talk about a proud moment despite being nervous and messing up a little, or maybe a lot. I played several sports over the years including softball, basketball, cross country, and track. I was one of those weird runners that not only ran the hurdles, but also ran long distance, and I loved it. I was never the fastest runner, but I tried my best and sometimes placed. Cheering was also fun. I really loved using my creativity to make the huge paper run-through signs that you don't see any more. I enjoyed being a part of the Friday Night Lights experience, with Texas-sized homecoming mums and all. However, cheering also introduced me to older girls and their influence in my life from an early age. Most of them had boyfriends, and I always felt the need to have one too. In a way I used boys to try and feel the emptiness in my heart after Tara moved away, but they only made it worse. Looking back, I could have done without the stress of a boyfriend nearly my entire teenage life. I had more than enough on my plate, but for some reason it was never enough.

Despite being super busy with all my activities, a part-time job, and pursuing boys, my school- work remained a priority. And my parents say, thank God for that. I took all the AP and dual credit classes, woke up early and stayed up late to make sure my assignments were done. Many mornings my alarm would go off at 4am so I could study for a quiz that day. I was naturally driven and self-motivated when it came to school. I was organized and always prepared for the day ahead. I was a hard worker and wanted to do well. I strived to please not only my parents but myself. I was dedicated to making all A's while also juggling what felt like a million other things. My people pleasing personality was what probably led me to say yes to all the things. Saying no was difficult for me. Doing everything that I did was sometimes exhausting, but I continued to do it, not wanting to let anyone down.

When I felt the temptation to play smaller, when I made some bad choices that definitely made me smaller, I figured out a way to keep working hard. My hard work put me in the running for Valedictorian of my high school class. And when it came down to finding out if I was #1 or #2, my school counselor made my friend and I sit and calculate and recalculate our own grades. I ended up being Valedictorian by just the smallest 4 thousandths of a point. It was absolutely wild how close it was. Each grade truly mattered. All those mornings I woke up at 4am paid off. It was a huge accomplishment, but inside I still felt like I couldn't truly celebrate the title that I had earned. It's crazy how self-doubt and the opinions of other people can steal your joy on such a special day. I'm so glad that I have come a long way in my personal growth journey and no longer let self-doubt or the opinions of others weigh so heavily on my ability to feel happiness and joy.

When this farmer's daughter dreamed big, I never really dreamed of being Valedictorian. I worked hard and wanted to achieve great things, but I never gained the confidence I would need to accept that role. I was a little terrified at the thought of having to give a speech. Getting up in front of a crowd was definitely not my thing. In fact, it was my worst fear and still is today. During this time of both celebration and somewhat petrifying fear, I couldn't help but wonder if Tara had still been with our class, if maybe things would have turned out differently. She very well could have been Valedictorian. Who knows, we might have gone to college together, been roommates, and maybe even pushed each other to go on to medical school. She had a way of naturally encouraging me to do well and be more confident. It's quite possible that her still being there might have changed the entire trajectory of both of our lives. Having more confidence might have changed how I approached that next season of my life. Having her by my side might have pushed me to reach for an even bigger, bolder dream that would require incredible audaciousness. But God had a different plan and path for each of us. Moving to Mississippi gave her the opportunity to meet her future husband in high school and go on to optometry school, creating a beautiful life that I am now able to follow on social media. And I ended up exactly where I was supposed to be, pursuing my own dreams, learning through failure, falling and getting back up, and thankfully meeting my future husband while all this took place. I am who I am today because of all my experiences, and had they not happened the way that they did, I might not have the life I have today.

My high school years definitely had ups and downs. Those years were filled with lots of fun memories, but also confusing relationships, a few mean girls who liked to bring me down, typical peer pressures, and loads of insecurity. There was bad hair, sometimes really bad hair, braces not once but twice, and definitely questionable fashion. Like most girls in the 90's, I had big bangs and one too many perms. I tried to secretly lighten my hair with a product called Sun In, only to be caught by my Mom and taken to the salon to have it "fixed" with dark, nearly black hair. It was pretty awful, as I waited for the darkness to fade and my natural hair color to return. Being a teenager was tough for so many different reasons. Like a lot of teenagers, I was trying to figure out who I was, develop my own sense of style, and learn to stand firm in my core beliefs and values.

Sadly, I did not feel secure in who I was nor was I confident in my faith and walk with God. The standards and values I had for myself often felt different than some of my peers, causing me to question them. I went back and forth between living a life that glorified God and living life to simply please others. As I reflect on those years of high school, I wish the older, much wiser version of myself could go back and tell that young, less confident teenage version of myself that the things I worried about then just didn't matter; that those boys weren't worth my time or heart-ache; that mean girls were part of everyone's childhood, but wouldn't matter later in life; and that loving God and respecting myself and my standards were what mattered most. Had my faith been stronger and my walk with God been deeper; if I had been more confident in myself and less worried about the opinions or influence of others, I am certain that I would have been happier and more fulfilled. But we can't change our past, we can only learn from it and change the story of our future.

My past was not only influenced by my own struggles and insecurities, but also unfortunate life events that happened all around me. As if that season of life wasn't already challenging enough, our town and our school had to cope with several tragedies during my high school years. When I was a freshman, we lost 3 young lives within the same year to horrible car accidents. Our town felt shaken and cursed at the same time, as it was literally one shockingly announcement after another. Each one stung just a little more than the last. It was so incredibly sad. These were great kids from nice families with a full life ahead of them. The weight of it all was so heavy, as we asked why it kept happening. We had so many questions and so little answers.

Unfortunately, tragedy is part of everyone's life, and life is just not fair. As a teenager, I was forced to learn this harsh reality, and it still didn't seem right. During that heartbreaking year, we all came to the realization that bad things sometimes happen to really good people, and time is most certainly not something that is guaranteed to any of us. Time is a beautiful gift, and sometimes our time here on Earth is cut short by tragedy or disease. It was such a tough lesson to learn at an early age.

A few years later, when I was still in high school, my older brother was home from college and reconnecting with high school buddies. A fun night with friends changed in just a split second, causing one of his best friends his life. This friend was an only child and the life of every party, a guy that everyone loved to be around. The accident occurred on our country road, less than a mile from our house. I still remember waking up to the terrible news and I'm sure it still haunts everyone involved that night. What haunted me for years is that it easily could have been my brother. Any one or all of those friends could have lost their life that night. Many years later, my younger brother was in a horrific head-on collision with a man in a truck that was having a diabetic crisis. Brad's life was somehow spared that day, but looking back at pictures, it's unclear how. It truly was a miracle that anyone survived that accident, but everyone did. My family would've been forever changed had things ended differently on those two awful days. Other families have not been so lucky.

Even to this day, there have been many more young lives taken too soon in my hometown, so many for such a small community to have to endure. That's the thing about living in a small town. You literally know everyone and are often connected in many ways. When something bad happens, you know the person or family involved. You feel their pain and hurt for them like you hurt for your own family.

My parents are sometimes asked why God chose to save Brad and not their child that suffered a similar or even less severe accident in our town. It's a difficult question to answer as we've all questioned why bad things happen and why some families experience a miracle and others experience incredible sadness and loss. Why him? Why that family? Why this cancer, disease, miscarriage, trauma, or accident? Why another natural disaster or mass shooting? Why the endless suffering? Why now? Why didn't God answer my prayer, but answered hers? Why would a loving God allow such pain and suffering? Why doesn't He put a stop to it? And the only explanation that I have come to know is that God never promised that there wouldn't be suffering, and He doesn't decide who suffers in this very broken world we live in. He doesn't pick and choose who suffers, otherwise bad people would be the only ones to experience pain and suffering. He told us that "in the world you will have tribulation but take heart; I have overcome the world." (John 16:33, NIV) God says there will be suffering, but also says that "suffering produces endurance, and endurance produces character and character produces hope." (Romans 5:3-4, ESV) We have hope in our future with Christ, as He says, "For I consider that the sufferings of this present time are not worth comparing with the glory that is to be revealed to us." (Romans 8:18, ESV)

I don't believe that everything happens for a reason. I don't believe that God chose to save or spare each of my brothers' lives and instead chose to not save someone else's. I think my brothers were simply lucky to live through the things they did, just like others walk away from similar things and avoid an early death. I believe that pain and suffering, tragedy and illness are simply the result of tragic accidents, human error, bad luck or bad genetics, not at the hands of an unloving Father. Life is not fair and will continue to not be fair. What I do know is that God never leaves us. He sees us and knows our suffering and hears our cries in the middle of the night. Yes, he can still move mountains, but sometimes He doesn't move them the way we want Him to. He doesn't always take away the mountain, but instead makes it a little easier to climb and overcome. He places the right people in our lives at just the right time. He points us to certain scripture to offer comfort. He gives us a sign to let us know that everything is going to be okay. He places tools in our hands to help us recover, rebuild, reconnect, and renew. God can turn our ashes into beauty if we allow Him to work in us. Joy can be found in the midst of our suffering if we choose to see it. Looking for hope and choosing joy in a season of suffering and sorrow is the biggest test of our faith. Romans 8:18 (NIV) reassures us that "The pain that you've been feeling cannot compare to the joy that's coming."

Cheers to my teenage years that often felt like a roller coaster, filled with high peaks and low valleys. Fun memories with friends, going to state in marching band, playing the piano at my brother's graduation, cheering under the Friday night lights, and earning the title of Valedictorian were some of the wonderful highlights I will never forget. But there was also plenty of hard stuff, things I just wasn't ready for, traumatic events showing me how unfair life really is, and plenty of lessons and opportunities for growth. If I could go back and repeat those years (Lord, please don't make me.), I would definitely be kinder to my parents, spend more time appreciating and enjoying the little things, and spend less time worrying about what everyone else was doing or thinking. I would be stronger in my faith and more confident in myself and my worth. I would say no to the things I didn't love or wasn't great at and say yes to the things that really mattered; things that brought joy and boosted my confidence. I'm sure everyone would change things about their past if they could, but those experiences also helped shape me into the person I am today, so for that I am thankful. "And we know that in all things God works for the good of those who love Him, who have been called according to His purpose." (Romans 8:28, NIV)

CHAPTER 4:

FAMILY TIES

"Other things may change us, but we start and end with the family." Anthony Brandt

I dreamed a lot when I was growing up, but my biggest dream as a little girl was to have a sister. I dreamed and dreamed of having a sister, praying that somehow my wish would be granted. I just couldn't see how I could possibly go through life without one. It seemed as though everyone I knew had a sister, and I was the odd one out. It didn't feel fair to me that my brothers had each other, and I was the only girl. I felt like I was truly missing out on having that built-in best friend to grow up with. Oh, how I longed for a sister, begging my Mom for one even though it was no longer possible. It just wasn't part of God's plan. He had something better in mind for me, but I just didn't know it yet.

For the most part, my brothers and I grew up doing our own things. We stayed busy with all our sports and activities during the year, probably making my Mom feel like a taxi driver. But there was one particular season that really brought us all together. That season was baseball, rather softball for me. For several years, we traveled from one field to the next, living on hot dogs and Frito pies, cheering each other on. One summer, all 3 of us were in All-Stars. We commemorated the season by taking a fun picture of us in our All-Star Uniforms with our gloves stretched out. That was a really fun summer in Waco with lots of our favorite Poppa Rollo's pizza. I didn't love softball, and eventually gave it up, but my brothers sure did love the game of baseball, each playing catcher all throughout high school.

Despite not growing up with a sister, I did end up with two pretty cool brothers that helped shape me into the person I am today. I looked up to my big brother Justin, always admiring his group of fun friends and most of all his confidence. When he was old enough to drive, he would sometimes take me to school. I felt really cool riding in that red and black Chevy truck with the windows down, and the music playing loud. At some point he upgraded to a nicer truck that was later stolen from a movie theatre parking lot. It was the weirdest thing. My favorite year was when he was a senior and I was a freshman. Friday night lights involved both him on the football field and me in the marching band. My parents got to watch both of us perform on the field that year. When that school year came to an end, I had the incredible honor of playing the piano for his graduation. I remember being so nervous and also sad knowing he was leaving for college. He left for Texas A&M in the Fall as our life back home went on without him. I wish I could say that I remember his years in college, that we went to all the Aggie games and events, but I think our life at home was just too busy for that. I do remember him coming home once with his head shaved, and us attending an Aggie game or two during those years. He ended up meeting and marrying the sweetest girl, Kathy, who would later serve as my Matron of Honor.

My younger brother Brad and I got along great when we were both little. He'd often play "house" or even dress-up with me. I'm sure he hates that I just mentioned that. As he got older and more into boy things, we weren't quite as close, but always got along. He had to work much harder than my older brother and me in school as he had to overcome challenges like dyslexia. And after his accident and some of his injuries, he's continued to have to push through discomfort and frustrations. I admire him for all his courage and determination to overcome hard things in his early life.

Following my graduation, I went off to college, and a few years later my parents were empty nesters when Brad left for Tarleton University. Lots of things happened during his years of college. Justin and Kathy got married, Ted and I got married, and our niece was born. It was a busy time filled with celebrations and also some disappointments and tragedies. Life took a pretty scary turn during Brad's last year of college. While home for the summer, he was involved in the serious head on collision that could have easily taken his life. My husband and I had to catch an early flight home, as we were vacationing with friends in the Dominican Republic when we got word of the accident from my older brother. At that time Brad was on a ventilator and his condition was critical. That night before flying home, our group of friends held hands as we circled together and prayed for Brad. It was a touching moment that I will never forget. We flew home the following morning and got to hospital as quickly as we could. By that time, he had already been transferred out of the ICU and was thankfully stable. Brad's girlfriend Shana had arrived at the hospital as soon as she got word of the accident. I had only met her once, but knew she was quite in love with my brother. She never left his side despite his injuries including a traumatic brain injury that left him telling stories about being in the war. After listening to him and his confusing stories, we were all scared that he might never fully recover, but he proved us wrong. It took time and healing and multiple surgeries to try and improve the use of his badly broken arm, and he eventually quit telling stories about coming home from the war. Just days after being released from the rehab floor, we celebrated my parent's 30th wedding anniversary with a limo ride and dinner at a fancy steakhouse. We were not only celebrating my parent's anniversary but rejoicing in Brad's recovery. It was a fun night, despite the limo driver taking the longest route ever to get out to my parent's house. Brad still lives with some permanent damage from his injuries, but it hasn't stopped him from living his dream of becoming a farmer like our Dad. He and Shana were married in the years to come, and they eventually moved out to the country.

As I write this book, both of my brothers live just miles from my parents surrounded by green pastures, corn fields, and creeks. I have 2 fantastic sister in-laws who love my brothers well, one beautiful and incredibly smart niece, and 2 fun athletic nephews. We are lucky to live just 30 minutes from my family and we gather as often as we can. Our girls love playing with their cousins, having sleep overs at my parent's house, and playing out in the country. We are incredibly blessed to be so close.

Growing up without a sister wasn't that bad after all. When I was younger, I felt like I was missing out on something, but I think God just had something better in store for me. I learned a lot by growing up sandwiched between 2 brothers. I think it's why I became fairly independent from a young age. I learned to do things alone, and I still don't depend on anyone for anything. I am perfectly content going places and doing things alone. I also never really developed a competitive nature. Not having a sister to compete with was actually not a bad thing. My activities were very different and separate from my brothers, affording me the freedom to be my own person. I'm still not very competitive today as I run my own race, stay in my own lane, and only compete with myself these days. I also learned to be a caregiver as I would often do things for my brothers like clean their rooms, change their sheets, do their laundry, and sometimes even wash their trucks. I learned to live with boys, who are sometimes much different than girls. Growing up with brothers taught me how a girl should be treated. I watched how my older brother dated girls, how he showed love and respect. I learned to dance by dancing with not only my Grandpa and my Dad, but my brothers as well. On my wedding day, I not only shared a dance with my Dad and Grandpa but got to dance one last dance with each of my brothers. What a special memory.

So, I've told you about growing up with brothers, but you are probably wondering how my parents met and how our family came to be. God definitely orchestrated their meeting as they were raised many miles away from each other with very different childhoods. My parents met in their early 20's in Waco, Texas. My Mom had moved there for nursing school, and my Dad had also pursued his college education there and was working towards becoming a farmer like his Dad. They were introduced by mutual friends and ended up dating, getting engaged and married, and having my older brother in about a 2-year time span. Yes, that's right, and then within 5 more years, our family was complete. All 3 of us kids were born just 2-3 years apart, as they wasted no time starting a family. I think that's just how things were done back then. Women had kids much younger than they do today, and a lot of moms stayed home. That season had to have been stressful for them, as my Mom stopped working as an ER nurse, and my Dad was very early in his self-employed farming career. There was not a lot of money, but there was definitely a lot of love and a huge desire to create something they could be proud of.

My parents were some of the hardest working and honest people around. They raised us to be kind and make good choices. Maintaining a good name and reputation was especially important to them as our name had been around our small town for several generations. My Dad was a 3rd generation farmer, extremely dedicated to his trade, often choosing work over hobbies, but was definitely a family man. He was always present at the important stuff, like school and sporting events. Even a farming accident that left him with a broken hip, a cast and crutches didn't stop him from being at our games. I even wrote about it in our hometown newspaper that following Father's Day. My favorite time with him was our mornings together. We were both early risers and both loved to eat breakfast, so we always had a little time together at the breakfast table before the others woke up. He enjoyed making breakfast, and I enjoyed eating it. Whether it was eggs, biscuits, and bacon or a bowl of oatmeal, I ate it up, while watching him read the newspaper. He was the one who drove me and sometimes a friend to early morning practices and driver's education as I got older. I don't remember a lot of our conversations. His actions often spoke louder than his words, as he was a man of deep thought, hard work, and few words. Despite our lack of deep conversations, I learned a lot from his example. I am the hard-working, honest, dependable person I am today because of the role my Dad played in my life.

After returning to work, my Mom did a great job balancing her job as a school nurse, helping my Dad in the fields, and maintaining our home. As a working mom myself now, I can definitely relate to the difficult balancing act that was. I probably didn't appreciate her enough while growing up. Our house certainly felt like a home, and we always had home-cooked meals including dinner no matter what time we arrived home. As we got older and had more activities, sometimes we had to eat in shifts. At some point in the evening, she would announce, "kitchen closed," not wanting us to keep re-dirtying it. Like my Dad, she also attended all our events, and made sure we had clean uniforms and everything we needed to be successful. My Mom was definitely someone that modeled hard work, as she was never afraid to roll up her sleeves and do what needed to be done. Whether it was doing the dishes at my Grandma's house, cleaning up after a wedding or family reunion, cooking and taking meals to the sick or mourning, volunteering at school and church events, she was always helping and serving. She knew what needed to be done without ever asking. She was one of those people you could count on, and she is still that way today. I am a working mom and doing it well, because of the example my Mom was to me. I watched her do it well, work hard to make sure we had everything we needed with little help from anyone else. I watched her take care of herself so that she could take care of us. I learned to cook and clean and do all the things it takes to raise a family from my Mom. I definitely didn't show her enough appreciation or give her the credit she deserved, but I am forever grateful for the mom God gave me. I am who I am today because of my Mom's influence in my life.

My parents definitely put their heart into farming, family, and serving others before anything else. As mentioned before, we didn't travel much or have a lot of elaborate experiences, but they did their best to give us a fun childhood. We often did things within the state of Texas, and as we got older, they took us to Disney World and then to Colorado for our first ski trip. That ski trip was quite memorable as Brad and I suffered with extreme altitude sickness, adding all sorts of challenges to the trip, but it was still fun. When I was in college, my parents took each of us kids as well as a friend or significant other on another ski trip to New Mexico. I could tell all sorts of stories about that trip, as 8 of us packed into an SUV and drove probably 12 hours each way. We still laugh about that road trip today. Those trips to other states definitely sparked my interest in traveling and I am thankful that I get to travel a lot today. My parents have also become quite the travelers, mostly enjoying relaxing cruises that require little planning and thought. My Dad is still farming, but has decided to slow down some, so he has more time for their 5 grandchildren and traveling.

My Mom's childhood was pretty traumatic, as she grew up with little and tragically lost both of her parents to heart attacks or strokes when she was just a young teenager. She had 6 other siblings, and the oldest sister ended up caring for the younger ones after both parents died. It was a difficult time for my Mom as well as the rest of her family. She doesn't remember a lot, and the memories she does have were always painful to share as I was growing up and asked questions. She grew up Catholic and remembers her parents working hard to try and provide for their large family. A few pictures of her parents, including one from their wedding day were always displayed in our home as I was growing up. Her Mom was a beautiful woman, and her Dad was quite handsome. They were the Grandparents I never knew but wished I did. My Mom had incredible determination to overcome her tough childhood and create a beautiful life she dreamed of. She put herself through nursing school, living with some friends she met. These same friends were the ones who ended up introducing her to my Dad. Believe it or not, those friendships have truly stood the test of time, as nearly 50 years later, the girls she lived with are all still best friends.

My Dad's parents lived in our same rural community their entire lives. They were the grandparents that I knew, and they were very present in our lives growing up. Every holiday and every special event in my life included them. Faith, farming and family were the most important things in their life. My Grandpa farmed as long as he possibly could, and he continued to help my Dad until he became sick with cancer. Harvest was his favorite time of the year. He was at many of those family picnics in the field, always wearing his classic striped denim overalls and often a straw hat. He loved to work and see the fruits of the labor come in. In addition to farming, my Grandpa was also quite gifted in carpentry and had great bookkeeping skills. He also cared deeply about land conservation. A memorable summer day in our life of farming was when he was driving my Dad's combine and it suddenly caught fire, burning much of the field as well as the combine. Luckily, he escaped in time and was not harmed, but my Dad's combine including his giant phone in a bag was not so lucky. There were always farming accidents, but this one was pretty unforgettable. That week a lot of my cousins were in town and everyone got to go out and see the burned up combine out in the field.

My Grandma was a homemaker her entire life. That was quite common for her generation. Her role was to take care of the home, the kids, and be a good farmer's wife. She fully embraced her calling and did it well. Their home in the country was one of our favorite places to visit. Thankfully it was only a 5-minute drive from our house. As we drove up their gravel road, there were always clothes hanging on the clothesline and a garden full of fresh vegetables waiting to be picked. She could usually be found in the kitchen, cooking or baking and would happily greet us with a big hug. My Grandma always had a fully stocked refrigerator in the shed, full of ice-cold Dr. Pepper. There were always homemade cookies in the freezer and a closet full of canned pickles and peaches. Peanut butter between Ritz crackers dipped in chocolate were her cookie specialty, and we loved them right out of the freezer. There was so much familiarity in their house. Everything was the same, even the smell of moth balls in the linen closet that we often played in and left a mess. She was one of the kindest, most generous, and happiest people around. She loved cooking and hosting people for meals. Her hospitality was one of her greatest gifts in life. She was active in our church, often visited people in the nursing home, and took meals to those who were sick or hurting. Everyone that met her adored her.

My Grandma kept a diary for most of her adult life, which served as a great record to look back on year after year. She wrote a simple entry each night that captured the happenings of the day. It often included the weather and what the crops were making, but also important events in the lives of her children and grandchildren. The treasured diaries were later passed down to each of us to be treasured for many generations to come. She loved writing letters and sending cards for every holiday often including newspaper clippings that we might find interesting. She even had a pen-pal in another country. They shared letters for years and even met in person. She was saddened to hear of her passing in her 90's. She never forgot a birthday and loved having us all over for celebrations with a spread of food and a homemade cake. Her specialties included turkey and corn bread dressing, mashed potatoes, sweet rice (the most delicious white rice laced with milk, butter, sugar and cinnamon), fried okra, and fresh cut cabbage slaw. Pineapple cake and buttermilk pie were also family favorites. She managed to get the entire family all together for several holidays every year. Her garage was often set up for us kids, and we loved putting on plays and music performances with our instruments.

Christmas was spent sharing the story of the birth of Jesus, playing Christmas songs on our instruments, and listening to stories from their younger years. She and my Grandpa were great story tellers, always treasuring our time together, using the time to make sure we knew their story and where they came from. My Grandparents were always incredibly generous, passing out special envelopes each year with money for our college saving accounts, a tradition carried on by my parents as well. After story time and gifts, there were often games of dominoes that went late into the night. The kids would eat popcorn or ice cream as we watched old movies. We'd make forts out of linens and wake up to the smell of bacon and sausage frying in the kitchen. My Grandma always made sure we had plenty to eat, always choosing to be the last person to sit down to a meal. Being Grandma was truly her greatest joy in life.

My Grandparents worked hard but lived well. They had a wonderful group of friends they enjoyed doing life with. They loved to go polka dancing on the weekends, and they were also avid travelers seeing all 50 states, as well as several countries. They would come home with slides from all their adventures and give educational slide shows with their projector. They showed us that there was a much bigger world out there ready to explore. Their beautiful photos made me want to get out there and see it for myself.

My Grandparents were quite the perfect pair. They had true love that definitely stood the test of time and hardships; a love that was pure and sweet, and definitely contagious. I remember when they purchased our living room furniture for us when we got married. They came over to our apartment to see it and my Grandma sat down on the smaller of the 2 sofas and said to my Grandpa while patting a spot on the sofa, "Do you want to come and sit on the *love* seat with me?" It was so cute. I loved watching them journey through life, hand in hand, choosing their love and devotion to God and family over everything else.

Their marriage was definitely an example of God's amazing love. They modeled this love in every area of their life as their faith was what guided every decision and every season of their marriage. They were active in the church as well as our small community and chose to live a life that honored God and served others. They prayed before every single meal we ate together, always counting their many blessings and often shedding tears. My Grandma's kindness and servant heart was a direct reflection of her Savior. She truly shined bright for the Lord. It was evident in every area of her life. She understood that all blessings were from the Lord, and she always made sure to thank Him for everything. It was part of her daily conversation with anyone she encountered. I can still hear her saying "Thank you God, thank you, thank you" even today. My Grandparents loved God, loved people, and definitely loved each other. They simply just loved life and lived a great one. They knew who their Savior was, and as each of my Grandparents reached the end of their lives on Earth, they were not afraid of dying. In fact, they were ready to go. They trusted God, knowing that there was life after death and that they would one day be reunited in Heaven.

My Grandpa got sick with cancer the year I got engaged. It was a rare cancer and difficult to find. By the time I got married, he had turned yellow with jaundice. Despite not feeling well, he was there on my big day, and we shared a special dance, as we had done many times before. He loved to dance, and adored teaching all his granddaughters how to waltz. He would often hum along with the song as he gently guided us around the dance floor, making it feel so effortless. Unfortunately, he passed away 6 months later in March 2003. Oh, how my Grandma missed him. He was the one love of her life.

She continued to live for many years without him, still wearing her beautiful wedding rings. When asked if she would ever be interested in dating someone new, she would laugh saying "a man my age is either looking for a purse or a nurse!" She didn't want to be either. Instead, she tried to stay busy. She enjoyed being a part of our lives and attended as many things as she could. She loved becoming a Great-Grandma to 6 great-grandchildren (more would come after she was gone). We were so blessed to have her in our lives, as we welcomed our babies into the world. She was so incredibly proud to be a Great-Grandma and bragged to everyone she talked to.

She continued to host meals and holidays at her house well into her late 80's. Eventually, she had to move out of her home in the country and into an assisted living apartment. My parents did a fantastic job caring for her in her final years, but her health continued to decline. We all spent her last birthday with her, and my girls and I went and visited her one last time on Mother's Day. In late May of 2017, at the age of 91, my Grandma went to be with the Lord. Despite our incredible sadness, we found peace knowing she was finally reunited with my Grandpa in Heaven.

Proverbs 22:6 (NIV) says to "Start children off on the way they should go, and even when they are old, they will not turn from it." I was truly blessed to have wonderful examples of marriage and appreciation for family growing up. My Grandparents as well as my parents valued marriage and family and wished the same for all of us kids. We grew up not knowing anything different, as this was beautifully modeled for us. They showed us the way we should go, and thankfully none of us have turned from it. As I've grown older and have experienced many years of marriage myself, I am even more grateful for the Godly examples I had in my life. Marriage is hard, raising a family is hard, but so is everything else in life. However, if it's important enough, you'll work for it. If you value it, you'll take care of it. If you love it, you'll treasure it. So, I'll keep doing the work to make sure my own marriage and family are always a priority.

I realize that not everyone experiences what I did growing up. Not everyone had parents or grandparents that modeled a faithful marriage or experienced family life the way that I did. Family is sometimes separated by unfortunate events like divorce, trauma, distance, and even death. Life is not fair. Our childhood is sometimes not what it should be, as my Mom is a witness to that. But what I do know is that history doesn't always have to repeat itself. We can decide that there is value in marriage, and family is important. We can do the work to keep our own marriage strong and thriving, providing that stable home for our kids to grow up in. We can make the effort to gather as a family, create fun memories together and support one another. We can carry on some of the same traditions that our grandparents started many years ago or start our own. We can share our story with our children and grandchildren. We can extend grace, choose joy, and create long lasting memories with our family, focusing on what is truly important. Mother Teresa said, "If you want to change the world, go home and love your family."

CHAPTER 5:

GROWING IN FAITH

"Faith is caught not taught." Jen Hatmaker

Having faith is having hope for the future. It's what helps us get through difficult times, gives us strength in times of weakness, and points us in the right direction, moving us towards a life of purpose. "Faith is being sure of what we hope for and certain of what we do not see." Hebrews 11:1 (NIV) Our faith is like a tree. It starts off as a seed that requires water and special attention to make it grow. It needs deep roots in order to be grounded. These roots make us strong and allow us to stand firm when we experience storms in our life. We need our faith to be strong in a world that tells us otherwise. Growing our faith is far more important than growing our success, as we are no one without our faith.

My faith journey started many years ago as a young child, a simple seed that would grow into a tree with strong roots over time. My parents planted that seed before I was even born, making sure it got plenty of water to help it grow. I was raised in a home where I learned about Jesus from a very young age, as going to church on Sundays and praying as a family was as normal as brushing my teeth.

Faith was important to my parents, as they modeled their faith to us on a daily basis. They, along with my Grandparents provided this wonderful foundation through example and provision of spiritual tools and encouragement in our life. But I definitely had a lot of growing to do.

My parents modeled a beautiful example of marriage and a life of purpose to us as we were raised to be followers of Jesus. They were married in the church that my Dad grew up in and still attend this same church today. Their marriage continues to be strong because of the rock they built it on. It's stood the test of time, because God remains at the center of their commitment to one another. They will celebrate 44 years of marriage this year. I am so proud of the life my parents have built, but mostly the way they still love each other.

The church I grew up in was at the center of our small town. Zion Lutheran Church was a beautiful red brick gothic style church, built way back in 1922. The people responsible for the establishment of this church were German immigrants who entered Texas and migrated to the rich farmland of Central Texas. There were stunningly gorgeous stained-glass windows and an intricately designed altar with a statue of Jesus holding out his blood-stained hands. It was and still is a beautiful church building today.

Growing up as Lutherans, we were all baptized as babies, and then later confirmed as young teenagers. After confirmation, we were able to partake in the weekly communion and were considered members of the congregation. Church was a huge part of our lives. My brothers and I were raised as regular churchgoers and participated in the youth group, children's choir, Easter Pageants, VBS, and Christmas programs. We served as acolytes, wearing special robes and helping with the service. There were potlucks and baptisms, weddings, and funerals. My parents were always serving in different capacities at the church, and we often helped or at least watched. Quite frequently we were the first to arrive at church and sometimes the last to leave as my Dad counted offering. We were sometimes at church several days a week, depending on what all was going on. When I think back to my childhood, the church was a central part of it. It was where we congregated on a regular basis, had community and built friendships over the years.

We were absolutely devastated on a Friday night as we got word that our church was on fire, another memorable event during my teenage years. Like I said, I wouldn't want to repeat those years. I was cheering at the football game and sirens could be heard as fire trucks raced to the scene. The flames were put out by the firefighters, and the building still stood, but the damage was quite enormous. It was heartbreaking. Over the next year, we had makeshift church in the educational building as the sanctuary was slowly restored to its original beauty. A special night during this time of rebuilding was a midnight Christmas Eve service on the steps outside the sanctuary. I helped coordinate this event and played Silent Night on my flute, while people lit candles and sang along. We ended the night with my Dad going into the sanctuary and ringing the bell as traditionally done at every service. It was truly a night to remember. My older brother and his wife were later married in our church, and two years later we had our wedding there as well. It was my home church and was beautiful and the perfect place for us to say, "I do."

As a Lutheran, I grew up memorizing important things like the Lord's Prayer, the Apostles creed, the order of the books in the Bible, the liturgy that was recited every week, but more importantly I learned right from wrong. Being a Christian gave me a moral compass, an inner sense of direction as I walked through life. But even with this incredible guide for my life, I wasn't perfect, and of course I'm still not perfect today. No Christian is perfect as we all sin and fall short of God's glorious standard (Romans 3:23). Thankfully God has continued working on transforming my heart, as we know that a transformed heart results in a transformed life. Romans 12:2 (NIV) says to "not conform any longer to the pattern of this world but be transformed by the renewing of your mind. Then you will be able to test and approve what God's will is – his good, pleasing and perfect will." In times of weakness, it's easy to be influenced by the wrong people and temptations of this world. We all sin, and fall short of the glory of God, but we know that we can come to a loving Father and ask for forgiveness and re-commit our lives to Him. What a wonderful gift that is. He knows that we are not perfect, as Adam and Eve were the first to commit a sin, causing this world to be broken as we know it. He expects us to sin, but also delights in us when we live our lives according to His Holy purpose.

I don't know if I really grasped the idea of surrendering my life to God and having a personal relationship with Him when I was younger. Church often felt like lots of memorization and repetition without a personal feel or application to my own life and the season I was in. I often attended out of weekly habit and not necessarily to grow in my faith. I felt like I was being taught faith, but not always catching it. I went through the motions, sang all the traditional hymns, recited the liturgy and the Lord's Prayer, lit the candles when I served as an acolyte, but didn't really grow in the way that God wanted me to. My Bible often felt like a pretty gift that sat on a shelf in my room. It definitely wasn't marked up or well-studied like my current Bible is. My faith journey has definitely been something that has grown over time, as I have learned to trust in the Lord and let Him guide my eyes, ears, tongue, and feet as it says in Proverbs 3:5 (NIV) "Trust in the Lord with all your heart and don't lean not on your own understanding; in all your ways submit to him, and he will make your paths straight."

When I went off to college in 1998, I attended a private Baptist University, the University of Mary Hardin-Baylor (UMHB). Yes, this Lutheran chose a Baptist University, and some people sort of questioned it, but I never really thought of it like that. It was simply a Christian University with a well-known and respected nursing program. During my first year I was required to take New Testament and Old Testament courses and attend weekly chapel. It was actually at chapel that my future husband Ted and I first met. There was also a weekly worship night with a band and contemporary music that I loved. I was surrounded by lots of like-minded people who were stronger in their faith and great examples for me. Attending a university that focused so much on building faith and leadership was probably the best choice that I could have made. It was there that I started reading my Bible more and really strengthening my faith and walk with Christ. Attending UMHB helped mold me into the person I am today, and for that I am eternally grateful.

While attending college, I was introduced to different churches in the area, a more contemporary style of worship music and different ways of teaching the Gospel. Some friends invited us to Temple Bible Church (TBC) in 1999. It was a larger non-denominational church with lots of college students and young families that attended the various services. It was definitely different than my Lutheran upbringing, but different in a good way. I loved the simplicity of the service which included time for praise and worship music, followed by the message of the day, which was usually part of a series and taken directly from the Bible. The lead pastor was amazing, and the messages were very applicable to everyday life. This church eventually became our home church and as I write this, we have attended TBC for 20 years. Our girls have been dedicated to the Lord, and we look forward to their baptisms in the upcoming years as they publicly proclaim Jesus as their Savior.

Sadly, as I write this our beloved Pastor Gary just reached the end of his 6-year battle with cancer. He was the lead pastor of our church for 38 years, and we can't imagine TBC without him. He led thousands upon thousands of people to Christ over the years, never shying away from difficult topics, always welcoming anyone and everyone into our church. My Bible is marked up, underlined, and dated throughout as a result of his teaching. He lived a transparent life, always pointing us to the Savior, even in his final days on Earth.

He showed us how to not only live faithfully but also die faithfully. As he entered the gates of Heaven, he most certainly heard "Well done, good and faithful servant!" Matthew 25:21 (NIV) The Bible verse that Pastor Gary chose to live by during his 6-year battle with cancer was Habakkuk 3:17-18 (NIV), choosing to be joyful even in times of disappointment. "Though the fig tree does not bud and there are no grapes on the vines, though the olive crop fails and the fields produce no food, though there are no sheep in the pen and no cattle in the stalls, yet I will rejoice in the Lord, I will be joyful in God my Savior." What a powerful verse.

I am who I am because of what Jesus has done in my life. The seed was planted many years ago by my parents, fertilized and watered along the way, but a lot of my growth and transformation has occurred in the last 10 years. A desire to grow my faith, have that personal relationship with my Savior and fully surrender my life to Him is how my faith journey has blossomed. I am not just a regular church goer, but one who lives her life in a way that glorifies God every single day. I read books that strengthen my faith, spend time in devotion and prayer each morning, listen to music that lights my heart on fire, and I strive to be a witness of Jesus in everything I do.

No, I am not always as bold or as confident in speaking about my faith as I would like to be, but I continue to push through my discomfort, as God calls us to be uncomfortable. We are told to go forth and make disciples, to be strong and have courage, to help the helpless and encourage those who are hurting. Over the years, my discomfort with public speaking has often held me back from praying on the spot or offering spiritual guidance to strangers. Just thinking about it makes me nervous, when it really shouldn't. I have always had much admiration for people who have that gift, those people who find words of wisdom and can pray from their heart on a moment's notice. And maybe it just takes more practice and even more growth that comes with time. I do find myself starting to share more words of hope and wisdom with my patients when they are hurting and discouraged. Words of spiritual encouragement are starting to flow a little easier from my lips as I become stronger in my own faith. The more I work on myself, the better advice and encouragement I have for my patients. Being fueled by the Lord helps me serve in a more loving, empathetic, and valuable way. My greatest hope is that when people see me and see the way I live my life, they see Jesus. I hope that my listening ear, my empathy and compassion, my comforting words, as well as my actions are a reflection of my Savior. My mission is to glorify God in all that I do, to see the world through Gospel lenses, serving and loving people. My desire is to have a joyful heart, listening ears with a careful tongue, and willing hands to help others for "a joyful heart is good medicine, but a crushed spirit dries up the bones." Proverbs 17:22 (NIV)

Our faith is important. It helps to strengthen us when we are weak, illuminate the path we should walk down, and provides hope for our future. I pray that your own spiritual journey will grow over time. I hope that you find a place to learn and grow in the Word, find community, but most importantly walk with the Savior every single day. I pray that you find forgiveness, an abundance of love and joy, and that your life is delightfully transformed by the Holy Spirit. God has big plans for you and "He who started a good work in you will carry it on to completion." Philippians 1:6 (NIV)

CHAPTER 6:

MY STRUGGLE WITH ANXIETY

*"Life is not supposed to overwhelm you at all times.
Life isn't meant to be merely survived – it's meant to be
lived."* Rachel Hollis

You would think that having a happy childhood, growing up in the country without significant stress, and having the ambition as well as achievements that I had, I wouldn't be one to suffer from anxiety, but I did, and I still do today. My nerves can get the best of me, stealing my confidence and setting me up for disappointment in myself. My anxiety typically shows up as fear; fear of embarrassment, fear of disappointment, fear of the unknown, and fear of loss of control. Sometimes the simplest thing like driving my car though one of those automatic car washes makes me incredibly anxious. It's true. I almost died in one of those things, so now my husband is often the one that takes my car to get washed. Driving down the interstate with a large concrete wall to my left and a semi-truck to my right, feeling incredibly closed in gives me that same feeling of anxiety, as I fear for my life. Being the passenger of someone driving in this scenario makes me even more anxious. It's that feeling of not being in control, worrying that the truck driver might not see us. Can anyone relate? I also fear things like snakes, falling off a mountain or losing my children in crowded places. I had all sorts of disturbing nightmares while visiting Yellowstone with family a few years ago. I don't think I slept a wink, fearing one of my girls would fall into one of those geysers or slip off a cliff and meet their fate right in front of my eyes. These are legitimate fears, right? I never clinched their hands as tight as I did on that trip as my heart was constantly pounding while also trying to enjoy the beautiful landscape around me. I'm not normally a huge worrier and I can be incredibly calm and patient when I need to. In fact, people often refer to me as such a composed and incredibly patient Mom, although my kids might beg to differ. They've definitely seen me lose my cool a number of times when my nerves have gotten the best of me.

Being around certain people or being overwhelmed by too many people or too much chaos has historically triggered my anxiety. Not having things clean and orderly tends to make me anxious. My type-A personality requires a sense of tidiness, organization, routine, and preparation to make me feel calm. I am one of those crazy people that will clean the house before leaving for a trip, and come home and immediately clean out the car, unpack, start laundry, and go get groceries before even sitting down. Can anyone relate or does my husband have reason to believe that I have serious problems? I don't like feeling rushed, I don't like being late, and I don't care for surprises as I am someone who likes to be prepared. I'll admit that I'm probably a little difficult to live with sometimes, but I like to think that everyone around me benefits from my somewhat perfectionist-driven ways. Things get done, we are always on time, and I am often prepared for anything. I will admit that I have definitely learned to lighten up and relax a little when it comes to a lot of these things over the years. Our house is definitely not perfect, the laundry piles up, and the car turns into a mess each week as we go from one activity to another. Having kids absolutely changes everything. I've learned to let some things go, not stress so much over the little things, and focus more on what's truly important. I do still strive to keeps things in order though as no one benefits from a frazzled, unorganized Mom.

You now know about some of my little fears and the things that make me feel anxious, but stuff I can often deal with, and not necessarily feel paralyzed by. But what probably makes me more anxious than anything else is public speaking. Like a lot of people, it's my greatest fear, something that definitely tries to paralyze me when I'm put in that situation. Simply put, I hate it. I know, hate is a harsh word, but it's how I feel when it comes to speaking in front of a crowd. Just typing the words public speaking makes my pulse rise, as if my body thinks I'm about to have to go do the very thing. I am an introvert by nature, so being an assertive leader or speaking in front of people is definitely not my strength. In fact, it makes me cringe. I would prefer to do almost anything than have to get up in front of people. I get unbelievably nervous just thinking about it and imagining all those eyes looking at me. Stage fright is definitely a real thing. I can be so incredibly prepared on paper, but then the moment I have to go up there in front of everyone, my body tries to completely shut down. The words that need to come out of my mouth can literally escape my brain as I start to panic. I go from feeling confident on paper to feeling like an imposter in front of the people I am speaking to. Insecurity takes over, and I have to fight every temptation to run and escape the feelings of uncomfortableness. It's the worst feeling in the world.

I have been a somewhat anxious person for most of my life. From twirling my hair as a child to biting my nails until the age of nearly 39, when I finally broke the habit; to turning bright red when in the spotlight; anxiety has been part of my life. My anxiety peaked near the end of junior high and into my high school years. For some reason, my confidence started plummeting and my insecurity and self- doubt started rising, causing all sorts of anxiety, especially when it came to doing things in front of my peers. When called on, I was that girl that on cue would turn red in the face, develop whelps on her neck and chest, and respond with a shaky nervous voice. Other kids would often point out the redness, asking if I was okay, if I was having some sort of allergic reaction, just making me blush even more. I would feel the sweat dripping under my arms, as my heart pounded in my chest, and my stomach got that butterfly feeling that made me feel as though I might pass out. My anxiety would often cause me to get headaches, a stiff neck, stomach aches, and a mouth full of canker sores when I was stressed out. As if talking wasn't already difficult enough for me, adding some canker sores made it even more painful. I absolutely dreaded getting up in front of class or having to perform with all eyes on me. Giving presentations was my worst nightmare. It took everything I had to get through them without feeling like I might die.

Despite being smart and hard-working, I lacked self-confidence, and I had a hard time acquiring that skill. I don't think I was always that way, but this insecurity definitely showed up as I got older and felt more pressure to do well. I think it also had something to do with opinions of others. As someone who thrives on positive words of affirmation, negative comments or lack of encouragement led me down a road of self-doubt. My 1st B in college was in my speech class. I wrote really thoughtful speeches, but when I had to get up in front of the class and deliver my presentation, my voice quivered, I looked down too much, and I didn't project well because I was nervous. Despite practice and preparation, I probably looked a hot mess. My professor was not impressed. Instead of encouraging me and coaching me up, he made me feel somewhat like a failure. Some of my nursing professors treated me the same way when it came to presentations. Instead of fueling me with positive words of encouragement, they made me feel even more nervous and insecure in my skills. They made me question my goal of becoming a nurse, all for being a little anxious. I mean, how was I supposed to start an IV on a real person if I couldn't show my professor how to do it without my hands shaking? Would I ever be able to walk into a patient's room with confidence and perform the necessary skills to be a nurse? Would I always be so nervous when someone was watching me? My professors definitely had a way of making me feel incredibly small and intimidated. One professor in particular made me almost quit nursing school. She made me feel so inadequate, not smart enough to be a nurse. I think she thought by being hard on me, it would push me to toughen up, study harder, and practice until I became proficient. But in my case, it did nothing but bring me to tears on a regular basis.

It's crazy how certain people can do that to you, while others teach and mentor in a way that empowers you and encourages you. I have definitely made it my personal mission to inspire and encourage others and instill a sense of confidence instead of making them feel anxious or discouraged. Positive words of affirmation go a long way. It's okay to be nervous as long as you have the desire to get better. It's okay if you don't do something perfectly the first time, because there's always room for improvement. No one is perfect. I think maybe God placed some of these tough people in my life like a basketball coach in high school, the mean girls that stole my joy, the speech and nursing professors that intimidated me, and several others to not only test my strength and endurance, but to show me how not to be. He also placed really awesome people in my life at just the right time to encourage me, lift me up, and show me how to be a person that inspires and motivates others. I've had some very influential people in my life in the last 10 years who have truly made me want to be a better person. I am more confident now that I have ever been thanks to their inspiring example, wisdom, and encouragement. But it definitely took a long time for me to get to this place.

Despite my incredible discomfort in certain situations growing up, I never sought out medication or help with anxiety or my fear of public speaking. I'm not even sure I knew it was an option at that time, as we weren't exactly a family that ran to the doctor for everything. My Dad was also somewhat of an introvert, and my Mom would get nervous speaking in front of crowds, so I just walked through life thinking it was pretty normal. I mean, lots of people don't love public speaking, right? I sure did want to be better at it though. I hated turning red and feeling like my heart might beat out of my chest. I wanted to feel more secure and to be able to speak up for myself. I hated that feeling of incompetency, insecurity, self- doubt, and disappointment. I wanted to come across as the smart, prepared, ambitious, hard-working person I was, and not simply look unqualified and unprepared. I didn't want to suffer from anxiety for the rest of my life and certainly didn't want it to hold me back from living my life and making my dreams a reality.

As much as I wanted to wish away the anxiety and become a stronger, more confident version of myself, it honestly took years and years of work to get where I am today. And I still have a long way to go before you'll see me speaking on stages. Obviously, I survived nursing school and went on to be a nurse and then a nurse practitioner, but my anxiety and fear of public speaking never went away. Anxiety has continued to show up in nerve-racking situations and around certain people. I have often just tried to avoid those situations that make me nervous and anxious. I have also coped in ways that are not the healthiest. I chewed on my nails for years, often without even realizing it. It was a nervous bad habit that I hated but had the hardest time quitting. I tried to quit on numerous occasions, always returning to the self-destructive habit. That is until I had a sweet older, and quite beautiful patient of mine grab my hand and tell me one day that I was way too pretty to bite my nails. For some reason that comment stuck with me that day, and I decided once and for all that I could quit, and I did after challenging myself to not bite my nails for 90 days. I quit the nervous habit over a year ago, and I haven't gone back. It's been a huge accomplishment and confidence-booster for me. Caring for and painting my nails is now part of my routine each week. It requires time and effort, but I am determined to never go back to the bad habit that consumed my life for years.

We all deal with stress and anxiety in various ways. It's estimated that at least 25% of us bite our nails. We also turn to food, alcohol, or even worse things to cope with the stress of the day. These quick fixes never result in long lasting results, and often just leave us feeling worse. Yes, that glass of wine at the end of the day sure does temporarily numb the stressors of life, and that bag of gummy bears sure does taste good in the moment, but there are not enough glasses of wine, bags of gummy bears, lattes or other ways of coping to transform you into a better, happier, less anxious, and more fulfilled version of yourself. A deeper transformation has to occur.

Finding better, healthier ways to manage my own anxiety has been the key to growing as a person and maintaining my sanity over the years. This is where my transformation has really taken place. These are the things that bring me joy, decrease my anxiety, and give me a feeling of harmony in my life. We are what we focus on, and I have chosen to focus on filling up with really good things so I can spill out to others in a more positive and impactful way.

As mentioned before, I am someone that likes routine, organization, and preparation. I have learned to start each day with an awesome morning routine that sets my day up for success. I wake up nearly 2 hours earlier than the rest of the house in order to have time to not only get myself ready, but to have time for things that get my mind right for the day. I make coffee, spend time reading my daily devotional, and do some gratitude journaling and goal setting. I love Rachel Hollis's Start Today journal practice and have done this for over a year now. Starting my day with intentional goal setting and planning while also giving thanks for 5 things that happened the day before helps me focus on what truly matters. After my journal time, I use my time to write or I get my exercise in for the day. This pocket of time in my day is like gold. It's where magic can happen, as I have time to work on myself and my goals. When 5:45am comes, I get ready for work, pack lunches, make breakfast (usually fried eggs and bacon with a side of fruit) and I start waking up the girls to get them ready for school. After Ted and the girls have left, I take our dog for a walk before leaving for work. This time is also precious to me. I often listen to a motivational podcast that gets me fired up for the day ahead. This morning routine has done wonders for me over the last couple of years. I truly feel that how you start your day can have tremendous impact on how the rest of your day goes. I now look forward to my 4:30am wake up time. Gail Lynne Goodwin says, "When you start your day with gratitude everything falls into place with grace and ease." I have definitely seen this in my own life. I love starting my day focusing on all the little things that bring me joy. I love having that time to pour into myself before I start pouring into others. I love a routine, not feeling rushed in the morning, but instead feeling fueled and prepared for the day ahead.

In addition to having a morning routine, music, reading, having a creative outlet and running have been things that have really helped me over the years. I love music, especially praise and worship songs. Hearing the right song at the right time is powerful medicine to my soul. I have several playlists on my phone and enjoy listening to them on my long runs. I often listen to Christian music, making running a time of worship, prayer and reflection. I used to be a creator of music, learning both piano and flute and playing for years. It was a fun season of life, and I often wish I would have kept up with both, but during college, I just sort of let them go. It was a busy stressful season of nursing school, and instead of using my music as an outlet for stress, I looked at it as one more thing to do. It's a shame, as playing music might have been just what I needed to feel a sense of calm. It's been so rewarding watching my oldest daughter learn to play my childhood piano, and she is looking forward to playing my flute as well. Music is such a gift to the people it serves, but also a joy to create.

I have always been an avid reader and absolutely love books. When I was younger, I preferred suspenseful or fun light-hearted fiction books. Books felt like an escape, and I escaped as often as I could.

I was found reading any chance I got. I now read non-fiction more than anything else. I enjoy reading Christian motivational, self-help and other non-fiction books that give me knowledge and tools to improve my life. I am a life-long learner, and truly believe that knowledge is wealth. I never want to stop learning or growing. Every book I read gives me a new perspective on personal growth, faith, and creativity. Audio books have become an enjoyable addition as well, since I can listen while running or doing chores around the house. I like being able to multi-task and consume several books a month, in addition to listening to daily podcasts. In 2018, I stumbled upon several inspiring podcasts that have literally changed my life. After a hard season of Ted going back to school for his doctorate and other stressors, this was just what I needed to put wind back in my sails. As I started consuming these podcasts and doing my gratitude journaling and goal setting, my mindset gradually shifted to a more positive, growth-minded one. What you consume can totally change your mind and change your life. I am proof of that. It led me to writing this book and pursuing other writing opportunities that have required an incredible amount of courage and confidence.

Exploring my creative side has also been a great outlet for stress and anxiety. From writing to photography, blogging, scrapbooking, to organizing and decorating our home, I have always loved creating beautiful things. When I was younger, all I needed was paper and a pencil and I could go to town. I wrote any chance I got even if it was just writing letters to friends or my long-time pen-pal, or hand-written thank you cards that my grandparents treasured. As much as I loved writing and being creative, I didn't choose a career that allowed me to express myself in a creative way. Instead I followed my childhood dream of becoming a nurse, choosing to serve people in their most vulnerable times. While working as a nurse, I realized how much I missed writing and wanted more creativity in my life. In my late 20's I started scrapbooking all our trips and also started a blog as a creative outlet for myself. I loved blogging about our weekly happenings, sharing photos with mostly family and friends. I wrote about my struggle with infertility, then my pregnancies, and eventually about our 2 girls. It was fun, and even though not too many people read my blog posts, it gave me a chance to write and share my photos. It was really more about having a creative outlet than the people it served.

Being a creator has simply been a hobby for me, another way to escape my fears and insecurities. I have often dreamed of a job where I could be more creative, and I've often wondered what that might look like for me. However, I recently read in Elizabeth Gilbert's book Big Magic that "creating is just as much for the person creating the thing as it is for the people it serves." So being a creator doesn't necessarily have to be what I do for a living, but a creative lifestyle can still be a huge part of who I am. Writing and creating content can be an expression of my calling, but not necessarily my day job. I have created lots of treasures over the years that few people have even seen, and that's okay, because it was more about the therapeutic escape for me. Taking beautiful pictures, preserving memories in scrapbooks and photo books, as well as writing allows me to express myself without feeling anxious, and I love the process.

Running has also been an incredibly beneficial activity for me, and you'll see as you read the next several pages how truly transformational it has been. I could write an entire book about running, and I probably will. I started running as a teenager on both the track and cross-country teams. I even took on the harder races like the 300m hurdles. For some reason, I enjoyed the challenge and liked pushing myself to do things that others didn't like to do. As more of an individual sport, I was always drawn to running. I was never the fastest runner, but I showed up, I was coachable and willing to try my best. I was a middle of the pack runner, and I still am today. Running is incredibly therapeutic for me. I love that running takes place outside where I can feel the sun on my face, enjoy the cool breeze when there is one, and take in nature all around me. I also love the runner's high that I feel after finishing a race. I enjoy the challenge, the feeling of accomplishment. In college, I'd often go on runs with friends around campus. Running even became part of our life as a young married couple. We were super excited when our cell phones had the ability to play music. We would go on runs around the neighborhood and then later clock our mileage using our cars, since GPS didn't exist at that time. It seems crazy now to talk about phones not having music or APPs or GPS, right?

Running was put on hold for several years when I was pregnant and caring for young babies, but when our youngest girl was nearly 2, we decided to start back up again. By that time, smart phones had come out and had all sorts of cool features that made running more entertaining. Ted set goals to run a 5k, then a 10k, then decided he would set an audacious goal of running the Houston Marathon. This was his journey to losing the weight he had gained during our running hiatus. It was a lofty goal, but he was determined to achieve it. As he started running, I became eager to join him, as it gave us something exciting to do together. It became our thing as we logged our weekly runs and signed up for local races.

By the end of that year, we had run our first ½ marathon together in San Antonio, and the following month Ted achieved his ultimate goal of running the Houston Marathon. Watching him complete his first marathon was absolutely incredible. I was so proud of all he had accomplished in just one year with unwavering dedication and determination. He had lost a ton of weight and was prepared to run 26.2 miles. His parents, our girls and I, and a few friends were there to cheer him on. We tracked him down at mile 15 or so during the race, greeting him with decorated signs and cheers and high fives. It was just what he needed to finish strong. When he came around the last corner before the finish line, it's a good thing our friends were there to yell "you're almost there" and "way to go baby!" because as I videoed with tears in my eyes, I couldn't even speak. I was so unbelievably proud. He never gave up, he never stopped running. He put one foot in from of the other for 26.2 miles amongst a bunch of strangers. He relied on his training and inner strength to push him forward while his body ached, and he grew fatigued. Watching him do what so few people are able to accomplish made me want to push myself to run a marathon as well. I was truly inspired. If he could do it, I most certainly could do it too.

After his marathon, we kept up our running, participating in a couple more ½ marathons that season. Our fasted race was the Dallas Rock 'N' Roll half marathon. We pushed ourselves to keep a fast and steady pace throughout the entire race, crossing the finish line together with a time of 2:07. It was an incredible run, but I really felt it afterwards. In fact, I was quite ill, but we won't get into that or the fact that we had to catch a ride back to our car since the finish line was not in the same location as the starting line.

The following year some of our friends decided to train for the same Houston marathon, and asked Ted to train with them, since he had just finished his 1st. I so wanted to join them, but unfortunately plantar fasciitis, a painful foot condition kept me from doing so. I had acquired the overuse injury in my left foot after our season of running several half marathons in a row. I was really bummed but didn't give up. I tried to keep running, not wanting to lose what I had gained, but eventually had to settle for several months on a stationary bike. It gave me time to plow through lots of books, but my dream of running a marathon stayed fresh on my mind. I gradually started running again, but it took about 18 months for my foot to get completely well. It was a frustrating process, as I watched Ted and our friends get ready for their marathon, as I stood on the sidelines with my hurt foot. The girls and I watched Ted complete his 2nd marathon later that year. He ran the first 10 miles with our friends but started to slow down. He says that had we not been there, he might not have finished it. At mile 12, he was hurting and not sure if his knee was going to make it another 14 miles but seeing us and getting hugs from his girls somehow took the pain away. He caught up to one of the doctors that I work with, who was running his final marathon at the age of 60 and ran about 10 miles with him. Having someone to run with gave him the boost that he needed. Remarkably, Ted ended up beating his time from the previous year.

The following year, after painful injections and resting from running, my foot was finally better, and I was determined to check a marathon off my bucket list. With a little persuasion, I convinced Ted to run a 3rd marathon so we could do it together. If I was going to run 26.2 miles, I wanted to share the moment with my favorite running partner. Most people never run a marathon; very few people run 3 marathons in 3 consecutive years. Or at least not the novice type runners like us. The training is grueling and time consuming. Those long runs really hurt and take a lot out of you. But Ted agreed to train for a 3rd, because he knew how much I wanted to do it. A friend of ours even joined us, excited to check a marathon off his bucket list as well.

We did the work and put in the training runs, doing several of our long runs together. When it came time for race day, I was excited and nervous. Our training runs had taken us up to 20 miles, but those runs were super hard. I wondered if I would actually be able to run 26.2 miles without dying. I was determined to cross that finish line, hoping to run it in 5 hours, but really just hoping to finish. Ted and I ran the entire race together, our friend an hour ahead of us. It was the hardest thing I had ever done in my life, even harder than childbirth, if you can imagine that. When we reached the infamous "wall" also known as mile 18, everything was hurting, and I was fatigued and really needing a pick me up. I started getting teary-eyed since the girls weren't there to cheer me on. They were being watched by grandparents back home, and it was just too much work to bring them to our race. I didn't realize how much I would miss not having them there. Ted pushed me to keep going and not give up.

In Houston most of the race is lined with people cheering from the street or even their front porch. There are bands and funny signs and all sorts of entertainers along the way. Ted's race bib was easy to read, and random strangers kept cheering "Go Ted!" It must have been hard to read my bib, because not one person yelled my name. We chuckled every time we heard his name, waiting to see if anyone would say mine. Eventually some people along the street started yelling "go pink girl," as I was wearing hot pink. Nearly 5.5 hours later, as the sun was heating things up, we triumphantly made it to the finish line. It was a massive accomplishment, finishing that race hand in hand, and having big flashy medals placed around our necks. My step tracker showed around 55, 000 steps. I certainly felt it, as every muscle in my body hurt.

I was incredibly proud of what we accomplished, but because our girls weren't there to see us finish it, I left with a feeling of sadness. I was actually pretty bummed. The girls had been there to see Ted finish his first 2 marathons, and I really wanted them there to see their Mom run 26.2 miles. I wanted them to know that a working Mom with 2 young kids could have big audacious dreams as well. I wanted to show them that their future goals and dreams were achievable with hard work and determination. I wanted to hug them at the finish line and go eat pizza together in celebration of what I accomplished. As hard as that race was, and as much as it hurt, I was just going to have to do it again.

The following year, I decided to train for a second marathon, with the sole purpose of having my girls there to cheer me on and see me finish. Ted decided to sit this one out, but that guaranteed that the girls would be able to be there. This time I chose to run the College Station Marathon. It was closer and therefore more convenient. I was pleasantly surprised to run into my cousin Elizabeth who was running the ½ marathon. We ended up running the first 3 miles together before I started to slow down. It was incredibly difficult as I hadn't trained as well for it, and the race itself wasn't as exciting as Houston. There were long stretches of the race that I was literally running alone. At times, all I could do was walk. It hurt so badly, as I played every uplifting song on my playlist, determined to finish no matter how long it took me. Just over 6 hours later, with Ted and the girls cheering for me every step of the way, I crossed that finish line and greeted my girls with big hugs, and all was right in the world. Isaiah 40:31 (NIV) says "Soar on wings like eagles, run and not grow weary, walk and not be faint." That race started with me soaring like an eagle, slowing down to a run and then a slow jog, at times even walking, but I never grew weary, my eyes focused on God and this amazing body he gave me. These legs were able to carry me 26.2 miles not once, but twice, and for that I was so incredibly thankful.

There's just nothing quite like running in a marathon, or even a half marathon. As a child, we are constantly cheered on by parents and coaches and teammates, whether it is when we are learning to takes our first steps or playing in a soccer game or performing our first piano recital. We grow up constantly being encouraged, applauded, and rewarded even for tiny milestones and achievements. That encouragement and positive affirmation feels good; those moments of achievement give a sense of pride. Likewise, as an adult, there are very few opportunities to be cheered on. The daily monotonous tasks of housework, parenting and careers often go unnoticed and there is often no one saying, "way to go!" It often feels like running on a hamster wheel, wondering if anyone even sees you. However, when I put on that personalized race bib with my favorite running outfit and head out for 13.1 or 26.2 miles, I am cheered on by random strangers holding signs and ringing bells and giving out high fives. I am handed ice cold water by sweet volunteers that are giving up early morning hours on a Sunday. I see 70-year-old runners living their best life. I see the backs of shirts quoting Bible verses and listing the names of people they are running in memory of. I witness random acts of kindness amongst runners and volunteers as I painfully put one foot in front of the other for up to 5 or 6 hours. I hear my name being called out as I cross the finish line, and I'm greeted by more volunteers handing out medals and free bananas, telling me "way to go!" The race leaves me with tired aching legs, but a very full heart. Running is so much more than exercise. Running is worship. Running is community. Running is the biggest test of endurance. Running is fighting the urge to quit. It is giving it all you've got, whether you run, walk, or even have to crawl across that finish line. It is all the things we yearn for. When I say, "everything hurts and I'm dying" and "when's the next race?" in the same sentence, other runners get it. We can't wait for the next big race. We can't wait for the adrenaline rush and the feeling of accomplishment.

This is why running has been transformational for me and my emotional health. This is why I still run. This is why I eagerly sign up for races I am not even trained up for. This is why for my 40th birthday I am challenging myself to another full marathon. I love having big audacious goals; just signing up excites me. I love pushing myself to be better. No one has to understand it, no one has to care about it as much as me, and no one necessarily has to do it with me. It's my goal, it's my thing that makes me feel alive and confident. When I run a big race, all that self-doubt I struggle with all the time simply goes away, because I know I can finish strong. I've done it time and time again. And I will keep running until God tells me these legs can't run anymore.

Running is simple, meaning all you need is running shoes and the roads, but it's not easy. With each year, it gets a little bit harder, and I get a little bit slower. As life has gotten busier, it's become more challenging to find the time. But I can't imagine my life without it. Turning on my favorite worship music or podcast and hitting the pavement makes me feel alive and appreciative of the body I have. It is therapeutic in so many ways. I run because I can. I am not the fastest runner. I do not have the ideal runner's body, but I am still a runner. I do not train perfectly, sometimes having to skip a long run, but I can still mind over matter any race and finish what I have set out to do. I can still finish strong. One of my favorite Bible verses comes from Hebrews 12:1 (ESV) "Therefore, since we are surrounded by so great a cloud of witnesses, let us also lay aside every weight, and sin which clings so closely, and let us run with endurance the race God has set before us."

I still have anxiety, but I choose to not let it control me or keep me from living my life. There are still people and places and situations that make me nervous and anxious. I still sometimes struggle with self-doubt, as I feel like I am not good enough, not smart enough, not experienced enough, or not eloquent enough. I still turn red and sweat and probably look a hot mess when I have to speak in public, but I do it anyways. I own it; I embrace it, and often just laugh about it. And afterwards, I realize I didn't die, no one really cared that I wasn't amazing at it, and it actually gets a little easier each time I do it. Do I enjoy it? No. Do I volunteer to speak in public? Rarely. But sometimes we do hard things because we have to. Sometimes we are put into those situations and have to push through our nerves and just do the best we can do.

Over the years, I have found ways to feel less anxious and conquer some of my worst fears and habits. I have to take care of myself emotionally, physically, and spiritually in order to take care of others. Lots of people are counting on me. When I am not grounded in routine, spending time in the Word and journaling my goals and intentions, exercising on a regular basis, reading and growing my mind, and finding a creative escape I feel anxious and stressed, fatigued and burned out. When I am not filling up my cup, I find that I have much less to pour into others.

You might also be one to suffer from social anxiety and self-doubt, or maybe depression, grief or anger. It is important to find healthy ways to cope in order to find harmony in your life and thrive. Sometimes you have to create your own joy, instead of waiting for things to get easier, happier, or more fulfilling. You have to push yourself to get started, take that first step, try new things, and see what works for you. Your things might be different than my things, but what's important is that you find what works for you. You might not enjoy running, but Cross-fit or hiking might be your thing. Reading and writing may not spark joy, but drawing or painting, sewing, or wood-working might. Try new things; find time or make time to invest in yourself and your mental, physical and spiritual health. Do the work, fill your cup; see a therapist if you need to. Don't live with constant worry and fear, anger or sadness. Don't merely survive life, avoiding everything that makes you feel anxious, but figure out how to grow and flourish. Don't let fear and self-doubt stop you from being the person that God has made you to be. Don't let anxiety be the thing that holds you back from a more fulfilling and purposeful life.

I continue to be a work in progress as I journey through life, constantly looking to learn and grow and become a less anxious version of myself. Our fear can steal our confidence, take away our courage, and rob us of our dreams if we let it. We read over and over again in the Bible to cast out our anxiety, our worries, and fears; to be strong and courageous. I often run by a large rock in the park with the summarized verse "Do not be anxious. Pray to the Lord and feel His love surround you." (Philippians 4:6-7) I love this quiet wooded area in the park and often stop to breathe and feel God's presence. I am slowly learning to be a stronger, braver, more confident version of myself. It takes work, but I am worth the work. I've also come to the realization that we are all created with unique gifts and talents that can be used to glorify God. I can look at my social anxiety as a weakness and focus on the notion that I may never lead a team or get up on stage and speak in front of hundreds of people. Or I can focus on my strengths. I am an exceptional listener, I am incredibly patient, and I can effectively communicate one-on-one with my patients, providing empathy and support. I can help train students by being positive and encouraging. I am exceptionally organized, thoughtful and kind. I can quietly inspire and encourage people through my writing and actions. We are what we focus on, so let's focus on our strengths.

CHAPTER 7:

DOG TALES

"A dog is the only thing on earth that loves you more than he loves himself." Josh Billings

I can't talk about my journey with anxiety without mentioning my fur babies, as they have brought me so much joy and comfort over the years. Dogs are smart, happy, and extremely affectionate animals. They can offer incredible companionship, unconditional love, and emotional support for someone that suffers with anxiety, and my dogs have definitely done that for me. In fact, certain breeds of dogs are actually trained to be emotional support dogs and service dogs for this very reason.

A walk around the block with my dog listening to music or a podcast is free therapy. Sunshine, uplifting music, moving my body, and seeing that tail wagging can be an instant mood changer. And I often need this therapy 3 times a day. I need these walks as much as my dog needs the exercise, and I look forward to them every day. Just petting and loving on my furry babies can instantly lift my mood, take away my stress or anxiety, and make me smile. Over the years, we have brought home 4 very different puppies, each one adding tremendous value to our life.

In my last year of college, as I was quite stressed out with nursing school, I decided we needed a dog of our own. Ted and I had been dating for a couple of years, and somehow, I convinced him to go along with my dog search. Several of our friends had gotten Labrador retrievers for hunting, but I was more interested in a fluffy snuggly dog. I didn't grow up having dogs in the house but loved the idea of a furry indoor companion to love on. If I was going to have a dog, it was definitely going to be a well-loved member of the family. I started reading ads in the paper and came across an ad for a Bichon Frise puppy. After doing a little research, I immediately fell in love. We went to look at the remaining puppies and of course I fell head over heels for these adorable white fluffy babies. We took home one of the last remaining puppies, Ted spending several hundred dollars of his hard-earned money as a college student as a gift to me and named him Bailey.

Bailey lived at Ted's college rent house until we eventually got married, as I was still living on campus because of my scholarship. He was an adorable mess. He was basically our first child, as we learned to care for what ended up being a very needy dog. He was spoiled rotten and quite stubborn. He taught us a lot about being parents before we were even close to being parents. When he was about a year old, he started having seizures that grew worse over time. He'd often wake us up in the middle of the night convulsing in his kennel and then he'd urinate all over himself. Those nights were exhausting as we'd get up and give him a bath and offer comfort until he settled down. Medications helped to control his epilepsy for a while, but eventually stopped working and caused him to go into organ failure. It was sad watching him decline. He went from being able to sit on his bottom and "beg" in the cutest way to barely being able to walk.

In his last year of life, we added another cute white puppy to our family. We, and when I say we I mean I, thought it might help to give him a friend and also help us transition as we knew Bailey wasn't going to live much longer. Shelby was a West Highland Terrier. She was the tiniest thing when we brought her home, fitting inside the palm of our hand. She and Bailey became good friends and loved running in and out of the doggie door of our first house. We had a love-hate relationship with that doggie door. We'd often come home to muddy paws all over the floor and furniture if it rained, and one time we came home to a dead bird on the living room floor. There might have been a rat too. But at least we never found a snake! As Bailey's health deteriorated, we ultimately had to make the heart-breaking decision to say goodbye. He wasn't even 5 years old. It was a really sad day for us.

Unfortunately, Shelby's health was not much better than Bailey's. We learned that apparently white dogs do not have the greatest health, or maybe we just had really bad luck with them. She ended up with dry-eye syndrome and horrible skin allergies early in her life. We went back and forth to Austin seeing dog specialists for all her medical conditions. It was pretty costly, but we loved our dogs like they were children. We spent a small fortune trying to save one of her eyes, a phone call Ted will never forget, but it was really a lost cause, as her eyes remained a huge problem. We were constantly applying eye ointments, doing allergy shots and pills, but between her eye condition and her skin, she was always miserable. She ended up blind.

In her final year of life, I did what any dog lover would do, and got another puppy. I was early in my 1st pregnancy and knew that Shelby wasn't going to live much longer, so I wanted another dog before the baby came. I am not sure how I convinced Ted to get another dog, after what we had already been through. Maybe he felt like it was a battle he couldn't win with his pregnant wife. Nonetheless, we went and looked at miniature dachshunds and fell in love with a playful long haired brindle colored baby. He was not white, and that was all that mattered. We considered the girl puppy that looked just like him, but after watching her put up a huge fight over being bathed and pooping all over the breeder, we chose the boy. He came home with us and was introduced to sweet Shelby. We named him Cooper, and he miraculously turned out to be a healthy, low maintenance dog. We made our 2nd heartbreaking decision to say goodbye to Shelby later that year. She was miserable, and we just couldn't watch her suffer anymore. We had done everything we possibly could to improve her quality of life, and she just wasn't comfortable anymore. We wondered if we would ever have a dog actually live a long, full life.

Cooper was our only dog for many years. He was such as sweet little boy. He happily greeted each girl as they were brought home from the hospital. He was their dog, and they were his girls. He was a great family dog, and the girls absolutely adored him. His little 9-pound frame loved running up and down our fence and barking at all the animals behind our house. We frequently had goats, cows, deer and other animals that would pass by our fence, and Cooper would get quite the work out chasing them down. There was one special day where a baby goat was abandoned near our fence, and we rescued it and cared for it for most of the day. We took turns holding it and loving on it before finally returning it to the owner. Cooper was quite happy when the goat was gone. He didn't like sharing the attention. However, that day with the baby goat was one of my most favorite days as a family.

When Cooper was nearly 9, the girls and I decided to go look at some Goldendoodle puppies that a friend recommended. They had never gotten to pick out a pet, and it just felt like the right time to add another dog. They were so excited to choose a female puppy. Ted didn't join us, as he had a lot going on, but he did sort of give me the okay to bring home another puppy. Bless him for never telling me no. I'll never forget watching the girls sit there with little puppies crawling all over them. Talk about cuteness overload. That day, we picked out a sweet black puppy, and a couple of weeks later, we brought her home and named her Bella. She and Cooper took a little while to grow on each other, as our Cooper was an older dog and pretty protective of his space. He was quite jealous of all the attention that Bella was getting and had no interest in sharing his food or anything else in the house. They eventually became friends and loved going on walks together. Having a new puppy made us take even better care of the one we had.

Unfortunately, we were heartbroken again, as one night, Cooper just completely vanished from our backyard. He was gone without a trace. It's as if something literally scooped him up and took him far, far away never to be seen again. We spent days and weeks searching for him, crying buckets of tears for our sweet boy. Unfortunately, we never saw him again. Whatever happened was not good, and Cooper never lived to see his 10th birthday. It was painful for the girls, as he was their very 1st dog that grew up alongside them. Not having closure was hard on all of us. God must have had something to do with us adding Bella, as we had no idea that just 6 months later, we would lose our sweet Cooper.

Bella was left as the only dog, but really more like a 3rd child in the house. She was still a puppy when Cooper vanished. Having her really helped with our sadness, as we grieved the loss of Cooper. We started giving her some freedom in the house, but probably a little too much freedom too soon. Before her 1st birthday, I found myself driving in the middle of the night to not one emergency clinic, but two, including one that was over an hour away. She had decided to chew on a remote control and then proceeded to eat two AA batteries. I feared the worst, and not wanting to lose another dog, I made sure she got the attention she needed. It was an exhausting, expensive night. Thankfully she survived the ordeal, as they were able to retrieve the batteries without doing surgery, and we learned to keep our remote control out of reach.

As Bella has gotten a little older, she has become a pretty amazing dog and member of the family. She enjoys her walks and has even participated in some 5K runs with us. She loves being petted and rubbed, so much that when you move your hand, she puts her head under it so that you will keep petting her. She can be trusted in the house when we are gone during the day, she sleeps by our bed at night, and she provides endless affection to all of us. Bella is well-loved, definitely spoiled, and I pray she is with us for many years to come.

Our dogs have always been family, and each dog has taught us in different ways how to love bigger. Not one dog has been the same, but each one has provided unconditional love and companionship. Our first fur babies prepared us for being parents, and Cooper and Bella have been fun, loving buddies for the girls as they've grown up. I truly feel that a house is not a home without a dog, and we will always have one.

CHAPTER 8:

FINDING JOY

"The way I see it, if you want the rainbow, you gotta put up with the rain." Dolly Parton

In every season of my life so far, I've learned a lot about what it means to find joy not just when the skies are blue, but also during the storms. As a farmer's daughter, I definitely saw what a storm could do to the crops and the ones depending on those crops for their income and well-being. A storm could not only wash away cash in the field, but could wash away hopes and dreams, joy and happiness. My parents took that leap of faith each year and had to choose joy even in the midst of unpredictable storms. We all know it is much easier to experience joy and happiness when everything seems to be going right. When there's plenty of money in the bank and everyone is healthy, when we have someone to love, something to do, and things to look forward to, happiness flows naturally, right? Other seasons are tough. Sometimes our situation, our circumstances and our emotions get in the way of experiencing joy. It's in those heavy seasons that choosing joy is so important. It's not the circumstances in life that create joy, but rather something we choose despite our circumstances. Having a fulfilling life is finding joy in the journey, choosing to see the good in every situation, reaching for gratitude, and deciding to be happy even in the midst of the storm. There is always something to be grateful for, even tiny joys in the midst of chaos. After most storms, there is often a rainbow if we choose to look for it.

When I was a teenager experiencing anxiety, loneliness, and feelings of overwhelm, I found joy in books, music, and movies. I escaped to a happier place in the stories I read. I listened to songs that made me smile, and I watched movies that made me laugh. I watched some of the same movies over and over again, like The Parent Trap and Pollyanna. 30 years later, I've introduced these same classic movies to my daughters, and they love them as well. Pollyanna knew what she was talking about when she looked for gladness in everything around her. She looked for the good and spread joy to everyone she met, despite her circumstances. National Lampoons Christmas Vacation is another movie that has brought me immense joy during the holidays. It's a classic that never grows old. I watch it every year as I trim the tree and get excited about Christmas. Everyone should have a book, a movie or a song that can immediately lift their spirit each time you read it, watch it, or hear it. It should be something that instantly brings a smile to your face, lifts your mood, and brings you joy. I have several books I've read more than once, half a dozen go-to movies, and plenty of songs that give me fuel when I'm feeling run down.

In college, I started collecting pretty little angel figurines called Dreamsicles. Each time I received one as a gift or came across one that was difficult to find, I experienced joy. I collected angels that were special and meaningful, representing important people or things in my life. The simple act of hunting for new and rare figurines sparked joy in an extremely stressful season, as nursing school nearly sucked all the life out of my body. Years later, after they stopped making Dreamsicles, my crosses became my collector's item. A wall in our dining room is now filled with beautiful unique crosses that I have received or purchased over the years. I find joy in each cross I hang on the wall. Some have extra special meaning, and some are simply there because of their uniqueness. Do you have any collections that were started years ago that bring you joy in looking at them? Or is it the hunt that brings you joy? I've encountered all sorts of collections over the years as I've met people. I know someone that collects old metal lunch boxes and has them displayed all over her kitchen. One lady I know collects a Starbuck's mug from every state she visits. Another treasures her Christmas cottages and looks forward to every Christmas season when she can display them all over the house. A co-worker of mine collects ladybugs that are happily displayed on her desk. We can sometimes find joy in the simplest things like a fun collection that is unique to us.

I love hearing about the various things that spark joy in someone's life. I have patients that light up with joy when they tell me about their hobbies or passions. One patient that comes to mind is one of those extreme coupon ladies that loves looking for coupons and getting things for free. She has an entire room filled with all the free items she has gotten over the years. It's all about the hunt and the excitement she feels when she takes home an entire basket of items for free. I have other patients that love dancing, traveling, hunting, and fishing. They can spend their entire visit talking all about the things that light their hearts on fire. I have an aunt that loves camping and traveling all over the country with her little dog. I have a sister in-law that adores horses. I have friends who enjoy Cross-fit. My parents get excited about cruises. My mother in-law is part of an organization that meets together and volunteers all over the state. It's a steady thing in her life that has brought joy despite losing her husband several years ago.

As an adult and especially as a working Mom, I have found joy in all the things that produce a feeling of routine and harmony in my life. As mentioned in a previous chapter, reading books, listening to podcasts, photography, writing, listening to music, walking my dog, and running bring me a tremendous amount of joy. Without these things in my life, I start focusing on all the negativity. I start to feel down, burned out, tired, frustrated, irritable, bored, and unfulfilled. Instead of feeling joy, I feel joy-less. But, remember joy is a choice. Joy is something you have to reach for, create, and engineer. You don't just feel energy, you have to make energy. You don't just feel joy; you have to look for ways to experience it. Sometimes you can find joy in the simplest things. Every Thursday, on my day off, I treat myself to a Starbuck's drink. In those 20 minutes as I sip on my favorite warm beverage, and often walk around Target, I experience pure joy. I look forward to it every single week. In the morning when I take my dog on a walk before work, I often catch a beautiful sunrise. In those 5 minutes as I watch the sun come up, I smile with joy, thanking God for a new day. I find happiness in clean sheets every week, a long hot shower, cleaning and decorating my house, enjoying a glass of red wine at night, watching old movies with my girls, and date nights with my hubby. I find joy in driving a clean car; traveling and experiencing new places and new adventures with my family, attending football games at our alma mater, and watching my girls do the things that light their hearts on fire. There is gold all around us, tiny pleasures, and simple joys if we choose to look for them.

In my current job as a nurse practitioner, I see up to 20 patients or families a day. I see people of all ages. I not only talk to them about their health, but also about their life. It breaks my heart when I hear so many people, especially older patients talk about their sadness, loneliness and loss of purpose and fulfillment in life. They've lost their spouse, their child, their closest friends, their purpose, their spark, their joy. They sit around their house or apartment waiting for visitors, waiting for a phone call, waiting for happiness, and sometimes simply waiting to die. In their final years of life, instead of making the most of each day, they are wishing their time was up. How sad is that? So often we forget that we have to intentionally do things to spark joy. We have to create our own happiness, look for sunshine on a rainy day, and search for that rainbow after the storm. We have to find community instead of waiting for people to come to us. We have to make the phone call instead of waiting for the phone to ring. We have to take up the hobby, learn new things, read the book, turn on the music, make the coffee, bake the cake, get a dog, go for the walk, volunteer at the event, and do things that spark joy. Remember, choosing joy is a choice. And not looking for or creating joy is also a choice.

We can complain about everything, focus on all the negativity, ask for a "happy pill," or we can decide to focus on what's good and what sparks joy. I love it when I visit with patients who are loving life despite their age or circumstances. Their face radiates joy. They love life, love people, and find joy in the smallest of things. They ask about me and my family, they compliment my outfit, tell me about their trip or their grandchildren, talk about their garden or their puppy, and tell me all about their love for dancing. Not once during the entire visit do they complain to me about their achy joints, the fact that their family is too busy for them, or that they have no purpose and no joy. What a delight they are to talk with and be inspired by. Just listening to them brings joy to my own day. I can be having the toughest day filled with the most difficult patients, and that one patient that is filled with joy can change the trajectory of my entire day. What if we could all be that person that lifts the spirits of others? What would happen if our own happiness and joy spilled out to the people around us?

We often find joy when we are spreading joy to others. A couple in the front of our neighborhood spends the entire month of November every single year hanging lights and decorating every inch of their yard for Christmas. They do a little at a time and by the end of the month they have created an impressive winter wonderland. They enjoy doing it, but mostly do it to spread Christmas cheer to others. Year after year, hundreds of cars drive by to see what they've created. Each year they add something new. It's quite a spectacular sight to see. Every neighborhood probably has a "Griswold" house like this, has a family that loves Christmas and loves spreading joy to others. We can all find different ways to spread happiness to others. And in doing so, we not only brighten someone else's day, but we give ourselves a feeling of purpose and pleasure.

Our greatest joy is found in serving God and serving people. We find joy in the Lord, our Savior. A life that glorifies God is a life full of joyful purpose. The word joy is found over and over again throughout scripture. Psalm 5:11 (NIV) says "But let all who take refuge in you rejoice; let them ever sing for joy and spread your protection over them, that those who love your name may rejoice in you." Psalm 32:11 (NIV) says "Be glad in the Lord, and rejoice, O righteous, and shout for joy, all you upright in heart!" And Nehemiah 8:10 (NIV) tells us "Do not grieve, for the joy of the Lord is your strength." As Pollyanna would say, these are happy verses in the Bible. Joy is a beautiful gift from God that can be experienced in every season of our lives no matter what we are going through. Even in our struggles, we can experience joy in choosing to trust God. Joy just isn't something that brings us happiness but can be a source of strength in our lives. We can even find joy in our sorrow for Psalm 30:5 (NIV) says "joy comes in the morning." Our suffering is temporary, but our joy in the Lord lasts forever. God is bigger and better than any battle we fight, any circumstance we are dealt, or any season of darkness we experience. Decide to choose joy even in life's greatest storms. Be a Pollyanna.

Allison R. Smith

CHAPTER 9:

OUR LOVE STORY

*"The best love is the kind that awakens the soul; that
makes us reach for more, that plants the fire in our hearts
and brings peace to our minds. That's what I hope to give
you forever." The Notebook*

By now you might be wondering how Ted and I met and how our
story began. I often look back at old pictures and reminisce about
that season of our lives 20 years ago and think wow, how those
young kids have changed, but only for the better. Our love story
began in 1998 on the campus of the University of Mary Hardin-
Baylor when we were both young college students pursuing our
dream professions. We were each drawn to UMHB for very different
reasons. I was attracted to the school for the well-respected nursing
program, as I had chosen to follow in my Mom's footsteps, dreaming
of a job in nursing. Contrary to my lack of confidence in other areas
of my life, I was quite confident in my career choice of wanting to be
a nurse and chose one of the best nursing programs in the state of
Texas. I liked the idea of a small pretty Christian university not too
far from home. I was so sure of my college choice that I didn't even
visit other campuses. Heck, I barely visited UMHB's campus. I

didn't know a single person there, but I was also excited about a fresh start in a new place, and I hoped to meet lots of nice friends. I was paired up with a roommate from Tuscan, Arizona. She was super sweet, but also very homesick, and after just one semester, transferred to a school back in Arizona. Fortunately, I had become good friends with other girls in my Hall, including Margarita aka "Marge", Jennifer, and Vanessa. Luck would have it; they all came from the same high school in a suburb of Houston. We all lived on the same floor of our Hall and hung out on a regular basis. After my first roommate left, I spent a semester living in a private dorm room in the Hall next to ours. It was when my Dad was helping me move to that dorm before Christmas break that Ted and his friend saw us and offered to help. We politely declined the help, but as Ted recalls this story, he mentions telling his friend that he was going to date me in the near future.

And as predicted, we started dating the following semester. Ted had been at the University of Texas in Austin his first year of college, but his interest and determination to play college football led him to transfer to UMHB the following year. UMHB was starting up a football team, and he hoped for the opportunity to play. Like many of the friends I had met during my 1st semester at UMHB, Ted was also from the very same high school. I mean, what were the odds of that? It was through them that I got to know Ted. We sat next to each other in Chapel, and I eventually told my friend Marge that I was interested in getting to know him better. She chatted with him and quickly found out that those feelings were mutual. It was almost as good as me writing on a napkin, "Do you like me? Check yes or no." Thankfully he said yes.

Our dating relationship started in February 1999. We spent many days and evenings walking around campus, eating meals together in Hardy Hall, and just getting to know each other. He took me on our first official date on Valentine's Day. It was simple, but very thoughtful and sweet. We road in his blue S10 Chevy truck with a stick shift to Austin, where we grabbed some Asian food to-go and picnicked along the picturesque Town Lake. We eventually ended up on the grounds of the state capital and danced to Don Williams 1980 release, "I believe in you." It was a magically perfect night, and the beginning of a nearly 3-year dating relationship.

Ted was not only handsome, athletic, smart, and hard-working, but also funny, outgoing, and adventurous. I was more on the quiet, shy, and cautious side. I dreamed of adventure but hadn't experienced much as a simple country girl, or at least not in the same way. He was spontaneous, and I was a planner whose fear and anxiety could often talk me out of my plans. Even our taste in music was night and day. I could rock out to some Point of Grace or George Strait, and he was more of a Dave Matthews fan. In fact, he took me to my very first concert, which happened to be an outdoor Dave Matthews performance in Austin. He was a confident, fun-loving guy from the big city, and I was an introverted, cautious small-town girl in my overalls looking for change. He was that adventurous, positive person that came into my life at just the right time. He introduced me to finer things in life like concerts, the Ballet, foodie restaurants, and things like olives. In some eyes, we might have seemed like an unlikely pair, but I feel like our differences are what attracted us to one another all those years ago. I was interested in his world, and he was equally interested in mine. We kind of balanced each other out like peanut butter and jelly. As 1 John 4:18 (NIV) says "There is no fear in love; perfect love casts out fear." Ted definitely helped me grow into a more fun, adventure-loving person with less fear and anxiety as our love for each other grew stronger.

Our mutual friend Marge ended up transferring to Baylor after our first year at UMHB, but not before she encouraged me to finally grow out my bangs. Perms and bangs were a thing in the 90's, but thankfully that trend had come to an end. She also introduced me to the idea of shaving not just my legs, but my hairy arms as well. She was one of those friends that every girl needed, and I adored her.

Despite her transfer to Baylor, we remained close friends for years. We would often meet in Waco to hang out, and years later, she served as one of my bridesmaids. After all, she was the one that set us up! Through Ted, I met other friends at UMHB. We ended up becoming really good friends with several other couples that made our college experience a lot of fun. 20 years later, Justin and Celeste are still some of our best friends. Ted ended up playing 2 years of football with Justin, and I was a pretty big fan during their 2nd season, but ultimately, he decided to just focus on his studies. He had hopes of going to Medical School and couldn't balance football on top of all his tough science courses.

Our years of dating were fun, but definitely during simpler times. Cell phones were still a new thing, and texting was actually a luxury if you can imagine that. We often communicated through old-fashioned hand-written notes and messages left on traditional answering machines in our dorm rooms. The only pictures we have from our season of dating were taken with an actual camera, as cell phones didn't have built-in cameras, and we definitely didn't know anything about taking selfies. We had meeting places during the day, usually meeting for lunch, and I always knew where to find him studying in the library most evenings. Spending time together became easier as we eventually moved into on-campus apartments, and some of the guys later moved into off-campus houses. Ted and a friend ended up renting a house their final year, which became sort of the hang out for all of us friends. The guys would often cook or grill for us girls, and we'd meet up for episodes of the new hit reality show Survivor. 19 years later, we still watch every season of Survivor, and our girls even love it as well.

During our time in college, quite a few of us friends went to work at a local country club. Ted worked as a bartender in the grill area where he got to know all the important people in town and developed some long-lasting relationships. I worked in the main dining room, mostly working fine dining and special events such as weddings and banquets. I really loved that job. As a waitress, I learned valuable skills such as friendliness, multi-tasking and prioritizing. These skills really came in handy as I became a "glorified waitress," I mean a nurse, a few years later. We also had lots of fun working there. After working a late-night wedding, we would all sit around and enjoy a yummy meal from the kitchen. Sunday brunch was pretty awesome too as we looked forward to omelets and waffles. Ted was a hard worker, often working more than one job so he could afford to date me and eventually buy me a ring. One summer, he went back to Houston and basically worked 3 jobs all summer long. We were both raised with incredible work ethic, possessing the desire to work hard so we could live well.

During my last year of nursing school, two unforgettable events took place. In late spring of 2001, a nursing student in the class below me went crazy and set the main nursing building on fire. She literally broke into the building late at night, spread lighter fluid all over the place and started a fire. We woke up to the news and saw our building surrounded by yellow tape and investigators. We were stunned. Nursing classes were held in different locations while the damaged building was restored. The guilty student was eventually charged with arson and spent several years in prison.

September 11, 2001 was also a day we would never forget, but on a much larger scale. I was sitting in one of my senior nursing classes as two planes hit the Twin Towers of the World Trade Center in New York City. Remember this was years before social media, so we relied on television for our news. As my nursing professor started getting word of the events that were transpiring, and that it appeared our country was under a terrorist attack, we were released from class. We went to locations with TV's and watched in disbelief as the towers started collapsing, knowing thousands of people were trapped inside. Two additional planes were involved in the attack. One hit the Pentagon, and the other plane was taken down by brave passengers to avoid an attack on the President. Nearly 3,000 people died on that sad day; we were glued to the TV for weeks. As I write about the 9/11 attacks 18 years later, I still remember the shock, the fear, and the sadness we all felt. We will never forget that tragic day in history.

In December, I graduated with my nursing degree, a semester before Ted and several of our friends. We celebrated Christmas together, and I was almost certain that Ted would propose, but he didn't. I remember feeling a little disappointed, as I envisioned us getting married that next summer after his graduation. But then he surprised me on December 30, 2001. He took me to the giant oak tree by the pond on UMHB's campus and played it off like we were going to take some pictures. He wanted a new head shot for some applications. It was getting dark, and I wondered why we were taking pictures at this time of day. I knew something was up. After all, this tree was known as the engagement tree. He eventually got down on one knee and asked me to marry him. Of course, I don't remember everything he said, but the important thing was he asked, and I said yes. The ring was absolutely stunning and unique. I was completely overjoyed. We celebrated by driving to Austin that night and eating dinner at P.F. Chang's, Asian food of course. The following year was filled with planning our September 7th wedding, Ted finishing school and graduating in May 2002, and both of us trying to figure out our career paths.

I truly feel like God beautifully orchestrated our love story, bringing us to UMHB at just the right time, surrounding me with friends that already knew Ted and cheered us on. Those years at UMHB were transformative for me, as I found the love of my life along with some amazing friends. Yes, nursing school was hard and tested my strength and endurance, but everything else about UMHB was gold (and purple…). Our alma mater continues to be a place that we love and support. We continue to be incredibly involved with the university, attending football games with our girls, enjoying alumni activities and giving back in any way we can. As we attended UMHB, we also fell in love with this area of central Texas, our church and community, and made it our home following graduation. Our love story continues, and I know it will be a really good one.

Allison R. Smith

CHAPTER 10:

MY GIRL TRIBE

"Many people will walk in and out of your life, but only true friends will leave footprints in your heart." Eleanor Roosevelt

It's so incredibly important to have a tribe of friends to do life with. It is what I craved so much after my childhood friend Tara moved away. She was my friend that felt like a sister, and her moving left a hole in my heart that was difficult to fill. After she left, my friendships with other girls in my childhood waxed and waned over the years. I think a lot of just spent so much time together, that quite honestly, we probably grew tired of one another. The down-size to going to such a small school with a class of 70 was that there just weren't a lot of us. Several people moved out, and not a lot moved in. The same small group of girls competed for friendship every year, some friendships sticking, but most suffering ups and downs. We still had a lot of growing up to do. When I graduated, most of us just went our separate ways, attending different universities, choosing different career paths, and living in different cities. A lot of us lost contact with each other. It was sad, but it was reality, and I'm sure it's the same story for a lot of people. Friends change as seasons change, life goes on, and so do we. Thankfully with the introduction of social media in the last 10 years, some of us, including Tara and me, have had the chance to reconnect online. It's fun to see how God has worked in the lives of so many of my childhood friends.

I'm grateful for their friendship all those years ago, but even more grateful for the chance to reconnect and encourage one another after we've had time to grow.

Proverbs 17:17 (NIV) says "A friend loves at all times." We all want those deep long-lasting friendships with mutual love and respect, we yearn for them, but it is not always easy to find them. At UMHB I had the opportunity to start all over. I didn't know anyone when I moved in. Fortunately, I found a community of wonderful friends that built me up and made me smile, friends I could not only have fun with, but be vulnerable with. Living together allowed for that deep king of connection I longed for. Conversations over pints of bluebell ice-cream (hello freshman 15!), lunches at the local burger joint or sandwich place, runs around campus, late night movies in our room, and camping trips out at the lake brought us closer together. I met some of my dearest friends there, girls who ended up serving as bridesmaids in my wedding. It was through some of these friends after college that I was introduced to even more couples like us, and we all eventually became a tribe of amazing friends.

Having this community of friends over the last 15-20 years has been such a blessing to me. They have filled my void of not having a sister to grow up with and have replaced that piece of my heart that left when my friend Tara moved away. Year after year our tribe has grown closer, as we've done life together and gone on summer trips with one another. We recently celebrated our 10th annual beach trip as a group. We have hosted baby showers for each other, shared parenting advice, and we've enjoyed some fun girl's nights with wine and great conversation. We have supported each other in good times and bad, exposing our vulnerabilities to one another. Life has been messy and even painful over the years, and our group has definitely gone through some difficult things together. We've experienced divorce, miscarriage, infertility, death, job changes, moves, and betrayals. We have prayed for each other, sent countless group texts to one another, laughed and cried together. Just as Jesus wept for the pain of His friends, I have wept a river of tears into my pillow at night over some of the things we have had to experience over the years. No group of friends is immune to the pain that life can bring. But God has done amazing things in the life of my friends, healing broken hearts, strengthening marriages, making things new again. We've celebrated adoptions, surprise babies after years of infertility, graduate degrees, and job promotions. We've celebrated little things and big things, counting all of our blessings along the way. I can't imagine my life without my girl tribe and their families.

Our husbands are friends, our kids have become friends, and LTD "living the dream" has become our motto over the years. We've run races together, celebrated countless birthdays with one another, and have genuinely had a great time doing life together. Within this group of friends, I also found my long-lost twin. All those years growing up, wishing for a sister, my wish finally came true. I was introduced to Stephanie several years into our marriage. We are basically the same person. The resemblance wasn't apparent to us right away, but everyone else saw it. When our hair was styled and colored the same, there was a striking similarity. For years, I was actually mistaken for her in random places around town. If someone saw us together or saw a picture of us, they truly believed that we were sisters, if not twins. I didn't have a sister growing up, but I definitely gained a sisterhood of friends, including a twin as an adult, and I wouldn't trade them for anything. "A sweet friendship refreshes the soul." Proverbs 27:9 (NIV) My soul is definitely magnified as a result of my girl tribe, and I wish for everyone to find this same community.

God created us for community, and it's so important to find friends that truly add value to our lives. Friends are the family we get to choose, so it's important to choose people who are doing life the way we envision ourselves living. Our friends have incredible influence in our lives. We become the people we spend the most time with. Just by being in the presence of our tribe of friends should make us want to reach for our best possible self. Finding friends that add joy to our lives, who are positive and encouraging, friends who build us up and not tear us down is important as 1 Thessalonians 5:11 (NIV) says "Therefore encourage one another and build each other up."

Finding friends that are living a life that glorifies God, friends that see the cup half full, friends that love life and want the same for us is the community we want to be a part of. If we're lucky enough, we meet these friends in college, or maybe at work or church or through our children's school or activities. Doing life with friends makes life more fun. We are not meant to do life alone. God did not intend for us to go through life without community.

And just as important as it is to have good friends, we also need to be a good friend. We must be the kind of friend that listens and speaks truth and wisdom; be a friend that prays for our friends and points them to Jesus. We need to spread kindness and joy, give love and encouragement. We need to hold each other up and lighten the load as it says in Galatians 6:2 (NIV) "Carry each other's burdens, and in this way, you will fulfill the law of Christ." I'll never forget when Ted's Dad died of cancer several years ago, and so many of our friends made the trip down to Houston to support us in our time of grieving. They took the day off of work, made the 3-hour trip each way and were there for us. In the years following his funeral, we have also had the opportunity to be there for friends as they have grieved the loss of a parent or sibling. That's what friends do. They come along side you in your happiest times, but also your lowest times. Ralph Waldo Emerson says, "the only way to have a friend is to be one." Be the friend who takes food to a friend that is recovering from illness or mourning the loss of a loved one. Be the friend who just shows up. Be the friend that simply listens. Be the friend that jumps in there and knows what to do without even asking. Be the friend that gathers the tribe. Be the friend that brings the sunshine, calms the storm, and finds light in the darkness. Be a friend to have a community of friends.

Allison R. Smith

CHAPTER 11:

OVERCOMING FEARS AND FAILURES

"Those who dare to fail miserably can achieve greatly."
John F. Kennedy

My journey of overcoming fears and failures and pursuing the best version of myself is probably the catalyst that led me to write this book. This is the part of my story that not too many people know about, and it's definitely the hardest to share, but it's the chapter where I grew the most. I am who I am today because I failed and chose to keep going. When my discomfort felt crippling and my failures felt like roadblocks, I toughened up and pushed through. Jackie Chan says that "life will knock us down, but we can choose whether or not to stand back up." This is my chapter of standing back up. I had to experience a season of failure in order to learn. I want my girls to hear this chapter of my story and know that they too can overcome bumps in the road as they reach for the life they dream of. My bumps were small compared to what some people go through, but at the time they felt like mountains. But what I learned is that failing is part of everyone's journey to achieving any kind of dream or success. We all experience varying degrees of failure and disappointment in life. Our greatest failure is not getting back up after being knocked down. And in the end, we only regret the chances we didn't take and the dreams we decided to quit on.

Growing up I knew that the only way I could succeed was to work hard and do hard things. Some things came easy for me, but a lot of things didn't. I had to wake up early and stay up late, study hard, practice and practice, and push myself through uncomfortable things. In a weird way, I enjoyed the challenge and the great sense of accomplishment for achieving something hard. From a young age, I forced myself to do those hard things that made me uncomfortable but gave me a sense of accomplishment. It was that achiever mentality that I had. Despite my performance anxiety, I sang solos in front of my church, I played at piano recitals and even my brother's graduation, and I played Silent Night on my flute year after year at our Christmas Eve program at church despite my sweaty, shaky hands. Speaking in front of others made my face turn red and my voice quiver, and I absolutely hated it, but I would do it anyway. Being a cheerleader required me to go through nerve racking tryouts each year, but I did it anyway. As Valedictorian of my class, I had to give not one, but two speeches in front of hundreds of people. Talk about my absolute worst nightmare. But I did it anyway, mostly because I had to. You see, sometimes we have to do hard things. And guess what? We are actually stronger than we think, and we are totally capable of doing these hard things.

As I pursued my dream of becoming a nurse, I encountered more of those uncomfortable speeches and presentations that tested my nerves to the core. There were days that I questioned whether or not I could be a nurse, as some of my instructors were extra tough on me, bringing me to tears on a regular basis. At times, I felt physically ill. I wasn't sure if I could do it. Was I pursuing the wrong career? Was I really cut out for nursing? Should I change my major? It was such as stressful time as I tried to prove my worth, keep my grades up so I wouldn't lose my big scholarship, and push through my anxiety and self-doubt. I relied heavily on my faith, reading verses like Psalm 46:1 (NIV) "God is our refuge and strength, an ever-present help in trouble."

In my last year of school, I briefly took a job as a student nurse tech, trying to get my feet wet with some good experience. I loved my job as a waitress, but my nursing professors encouraged us to get nursing experience, and it made sense. However, after a few days on a busy medical-surgical floor and an absolutely horrible experience, I basically walked off the job. It got hard, and I quit. It was humiliating. I had never quit a job, much less walked out on it. What was I even thinking? But without a mentor, very little orientation, and an overwhelming feeling of anxiety, I felt no choice, but to leave the job. I will never forget the mortifying conversation I had with the manager after I chose to leave. He chewed me out, making me feel like I would never have a chance of being a nurse, and if I did become a nurse, I would be a horrible one. Talk about feeling like an imposter. Just 3 years prior, I was standing up delivering my Valedictorian address, and now I felt like a complete letdown. How had I let my anxiety and insecurity take over? At the tender age of 21, I learned an invaluable lesson that day. Quitting was the easy way out. Quitting was telling my anxiety that it won. I decided that day to stand back up and never walk away from something that felt hard.

I persevered through my last year of school and finished my nursing degree thinking the worst was behind me. I looked forward to being done with school; no more pressures, no more stress. I was finally going to be a nurse. I had finally reached my goal. I could literally put the past behind me and move on with the career I had dreamed of. Or so I thought. I received my nursing pin in a traditional all white outfit, and later walked across the stage to receive my diploma. It was a happy day with friends and family cheering me on. It was the end of an incredibly stressful season, but unfortunately the beginning of another one.

I still had to pass the NCLEX exam to get my nursing license, and I had no idea how difficult that task would be. I assumed I would pass with no problems. I had done the work and made it this far, so why wouldn't I pass? I had already started a job in the Neonatal ICU as a graduate nurse intern and had the best teacher and mentor for the job. It felt right. I was exactly where I dreamt I would be. I was super excited about my future taking care of the most fragile tiny babies in the hospital. However, NCLEX did not go as planned. I didn't pass the first time. That's right, I failed. And it hurt. I was shocked and devastated and embarrassed. I had never felt such shame and defeat. I wasn't sure how to tell people that I had just failed this extremely important test, so I told very few. Growing up, I had been a high achiever. I made straight A's; I was Valedictorian of my high school class. I had worked so hard to get through nursing school. I had just gotten engaged to the man of my dreams. Life seemed to be going in the right direction. How could this happen to me when I wanted it so bad? I had never experienced this type of failure and disappointment, and really wasn't prepared for it. I wasn't sure what this meant for my current job or my future career as a nurse. Would I get a second chance? Would my boss understand? Was this really part of God's plan for my life? Did I need to fail at something and experience true disappointment in order to learn and grow? Or was this a sign that I was not cut out for nursing? Should I have chosen a different career? Should I have listened to the nursing professor who questioned my abilities or the nurse manager in the hospital that yelled at me and told me I would never be a good nurse? So many questions went through my head. I felt so confused and frustrated. It was a massive time of humbling reflection for me.

Thankfully, I was blessed with an amazing manager and preceptor who were completely understanding and extremely encouraging. I have no doubt in my mind that God used them to encourage me and lift me back up when I felt like I had been knocked down. They worked with me and told me to simply study and take it again. They had confidence in me and knew I could do it. I kept working as a graduate nurse but wasn't able to do quite as much. I eventually got moved to night shift which I absolutely hated. I had a 45-minute commute to and from work, and those mornings after a night shift driving down a busy interstate nearly killed me. It took everything I had to stay awake. I spent time studying on my own for the exam, and about 8 weeks later, I took the NCLEX again, totally expecting to pass the 2nd time around. Surely, I had prepared enough. Certainly, I had endured enough embarrassment in this experience of failure. But as before, I didn't pass. I failed a second time. Seriously? I was shocked and crushed at the same time. I was in the middle of planning our wedding, Ted was getting ready to graduate, we had our entire life ahead of us, and for some reason I couldn't pass this crucial test. It was the first time in my life that I truly felt like a failure. I absolutely dreaded telling my boss and preceptor that not only did I not pass the 1st time but didn't pass on the 2nd attempt either.

Once again, they were kind and encouraging, but at that point, I had pretty much been demoted, and my shifts were frequently being cancelled due to low census. I wasn't considered a graduate nurse anymore, but more of a nurse tech. They weren't really sure how to utilize me. It was humiliating. I finally put in my resignation, apologizing to a boss I barely knew, said goodbye to a preceptor I loved, and decided to take some time off from pursuing my nursing career. For the second time in my journey to becoming a nurse, I quit. I had told myself that I would never quit something again, and here I was quitting. Thankfully, I left this job on better terms, but it still felt like quitting. This was hard, and I wasn't sure if I even wanted to keep trying. I felt like running and hiding and simply giving up on my dream. I questioned whether or not I even wanted to be a nurse. I wondered why this was happening as I was planning the happiest day of my life.

I went back to waiting tables at the country club where I had worked in college. It felt safe. It felt easy, and I needed easy when everything around me felt hard. It gave me time to focus on our wedding, still earning money and still working with Ted. He graduated in May and started figuring out his own career path. We were both in a time of transition, and I remember writing up the wedding announcement for the paper, wishing I could write that I was working as an RN in the NICU and Ted was pursuing a degree in medicine, but that was not the case for either of us. Instead, I wrote that I was a graduate nurse (yes, 9 months after graduation), and Ted was working at Wildflower Country Club. I'm sure our parents were proud. It wasn't where I imagined we'd be, but I chose to put my pride aside and enjoy the best day of my life.

After our September wedding, I felt more confident and decided to give this nursing thing one more shot. After all, I didn't have any other options. I had this degree and the only thing that stood between me and the title of registered nurse was this test. I went ALL in this time, attending the best nursing review course, studying like crazy, and then took the NCLEX one final time. This was it. This was my last chance. It was do or die. I was nervous, but also more at ease than I had been the previous two times. Going in to take the test, I sort of felt a sense of peace come over me, like God was telling me it would be okay. Joshua 1:9 (NIV) says "Be strong and courageous. Do not be afraid; do not be discouraged, for the Lord your God will be with you wherever you go." I sat there in front of the computer feeling stronger and more courageous than I had ever felt before, said a prayer, and began the test. It was different this time. As each question popped up on the screen, I felt like I had seen them before. I answered each question with a smile on my face, knowing in my heart that this score would be different. And it was. I was absolutely relieved to find out that I had finally passed. I didn't fail this time, but instead I passed with the least number of questions needed to determine my fate. Persistence had paid off. I had conquered this huge obstacle that tested me in ways I had never been tested before. God showed me that "I can do all things through Christ who gives me strength." Philippians 4:13 (NIV) I was officially a registered nurse, and I could finally put this difficult season behind me.

I never returned to the NICU. It just didn't feel like it was where God was calling me to be. We decided to stay in Belton, and I wanted to work somewhere closer. I ended up getting a job in the least expected place doing the type of nursing I swore I would never do. It's funny how things sometimes work out that way. God placed me in the same area of nursing that I had previously walked out on 2 years prior. It was as if He was telling me that I owed it to that manager to give it one more try and prove that I could be an amazing nurse for my patients.

For the next 5 plus years, I worked on a busy, challenging adult medical-surgical floor. It was on this floor that I grew from an insecure nurse with a lot to learn to a competent charge nurse that helped train others how to do the job. I loved my patients and really enjoyed training students and new nurses on my floor. I enjoyed learning new skills, becoming proficient at starting IV's, and juggling all the many responsibilities that nurses have in the hospital. It was fun, but also exhausting. It was an incredibly stressful job, and I would often come home with an aching back and feet, and I would talk in my sleep, hearing call lights and dinging IV pumps, and worry that I had forgotten to do something. I took care of people in their most vulnerable state, following surgeries and coming in with serious illness, and I saw people die. It was really eye opening for me as a young nurse. I had huge responsibilities, and I often felt the weight of it all.

Thankfully, I had great mentors and friends on the floor and learned so much from all of them. Having a great team made going to work fun. It made those long days of turning and cleaning up patients and running around without a break more tolerable. Several of these nursing friends were going back to school for nurse practitioner, and the idea started growing on me. As much as I liked my job and the people I worked with, I knew I couldn't do it forever. I also had a desire to do more. I felt like I could be more on the decision-making side of things. I felt like I could provide excellent care to my patients with an empathizing nursing prospective. My nursing friends encouraged me to apply for the Family Nurse Practitioner master's program which would open up more opportunities to work in a clinic setting and take care of patients on the front end of things. I was a little hesitant, as I had never pictured myself going back to school, as it was hard enough the first time around, but I finally decided to go for it. I had grown a lot and was ready for a new challenge, ready for a new chapter in my life.

But once again as I pursued a dream, I met another roadblock. I didn't get in. That's right, my application was rejected. There weren't a lot of programs at the time, and the program I applied to was quite competitive. My undergraduate GPA was just a little bit shy of the requirement they were looking for. I knew it when I applied but hoped my nursing experience and other items on my application would make up for my less than perfect GPA. I was disappointed when I got the letter and felt the same feelings of defeat that I had experienced several years prior. Again, I felt like a failure. I wondered why God put this calling to be a nurse practitioner in my heart if I wasn't going to be able to pursue it. I was frustrated and wondered if maybe it was just time to start a family and give up on pursuing this goal of becoming a nurse practitioner. However, my friends and mentors on my floor at work would not take no for an answer. My boss, manager, and a current student in the program wrote nice letters of recommendation to the program chair on my behalf, asking her to please reconsider. I wrote a letter as well. It was a last-ditch effort to try and get in. I was pretty sure it wouldn't work, so I was quite surprised when I got a 2nd letter stating that my application had been reviewed again, and I was now accepted into the program. Talk about a happy day!

For the next 3 years, I continued working on the floor as a charge nurse and juggling my master's program for nurse practitioner. That season of life was busy, filled with lots of driving and stressful clinical days with a preceptor that challenged me to my core. Those days were often filled with tears, as I struggled again with anxiety and had to learn to be more confident. I kept going, kept pushing myself through the discomfort and challenges I met along the way. I managed to get to the end of the program and graduated with honors. We celebrated the achievement with family and friends, and I looked forward to my upcoming job promotion. Once again, I had to take a board exam, but learning from previous experience, I took the best review course around and aced my exam the first time. Things finally seemed to be moving in the right direction for my career.

In the summer of 2008, I started working as a Family Nurse Practitioner at a new walk-in clinic for minor illnesses. It was a huge change going from nurse to provider, but I was excited. My nursing scrubs were boxed up, and I needed a new professional wardrobe for the first time in my life. My name was on the bottom of the prescription pad, and I had my own office and exam room. It was exciting and terrifying at the same time. I was now the one making the decisions for my patients, and not all patients were kind. In my early career, my education and training and age were constantly questioned. I was often asked when I was going to be a doctor. I was frequently told that I looked too young to be doing what I was doing. I was yelled at for not giving someone antibiotics or whatever they were demanding based on their Google search diagnosis of their symptoms. My confidence was often squashed the minute I walked into the exam room and was met by a patient who didn't think I knew how to do my job. But again, I was blessed with an amazing boss and fantastic mentoring physicians who oversaw the little walk-in clinic where I started my career. None of them questioned my abilities or age. They encouraged me and supported me. They never intimidated me, but instead inspired me. And over time, I started feeling more confident, maybe even a little bored, and desired a more challenging job in a regular family medicine clinic.

I ended up being recruited by a family physician to come work alongside him in his clinic, the clinic I still work in today. I now work more on the front end of seeing patients. I still see them when they are sick or hurt, but I am also tasked with managing their medical problems, seeing them for wellness visits, trying to prevent disease by promoting a healthy lifestyle. And sometimes I have the difficult job of telling someone they have diabetes, or even worse, cancer. Several years ago, I took care of a vibrant, healthy young kid that ended up with a brain tumor and died about 18 months later. It was the worst thing ever. I learned quickly that cancer does not discriminate. Even kids get cancer and die. What a heartbreaking reality. Our training only goes so far in preparing us for situations like this. Delivering difficult news and counseling patients during tough circumstances is definitely a skill I've had to learn and develop over time. Having more life experiences of my own and growing in my faith has definitely helped.

At my clinic, I see all sorts of patients with varying degrees of illness, disease, and disability. I've learned that many diseases are avoidable with a healthy lifestyle, but unfortunately many illnesses, diseases, and chronic pain are not. I've witnessed people making huge steps to transform their life and get off of medications. I've also watched as people continue to self-sabotage, adding more and more pills, and finding a way to complain about everything in life. I'm truly inspired by the patients that live with chronic pain and all sorts of disability that is out of their control, who continue to be filled with positive energy and determination to do the best they can with what they have, while also spreading kindness. Their incredible perspective on life is infectious.

It has been 9 years since I went to work at my clinic, and I have grown so much as a nurse practitioner. I am doing the job I was called to do. I love getting to serve a community of people, entire families from baby to Grandma. It is so rewarding getting to help people feel better and see patients making positive changes in their life to improve their health. I have also gotten the chance to precept and mentor nurse practitioner students over the years, giving back to the profession that has given so much to me. Had it not been for my nursing friends, mentors, and preceptors, I wouldn't be where I am today. God definitely showed his presence in my tough season of walking through failure by placing the right people in my life as just the right time.

Over the years, I have learned that the only way to overcome fear is to push through it. Those times I wanted to quit and even did quit made me stronger and even more determined to overcome my obstacles. When I questioned my ability to keep going, I decided to push harder. When I failed miserably, feeling completely defeated, I picked myself back up and tried harder the next time. I realized that those "no's" didn't mean never, just not yet. Not succeeding the first time or even the second time showed me that sometimes we have to try and fail and try again. We have to choose to stand back up and work harder and smarter. Through those failures, I experienced incredible growth. Maybe I needed to fail in order to learn and grow into the person I am today. God gave me the strength to keep trying. Without hope and faith, I might have given up completely. I might have chosen to give into my temptation of hiding and avoiding instead of persevering. He showed me that "faith can move mountains." Matthew 17:20 (NIV) I also had incredible support and encouragement from wonderful mentors that kept my hope alive and made sure I didn't give up on myself and my dreams. There is no doubt that God placed those people in my life at just the right time. I have never forgotten the help I had along the way, and I have made sure to pass along that same message of hope to every student I have the opportunity to mentor as well as my patients who need to hear words of encouragement.

I am still not great at public speaking, as it still remains my biggest fear and tallest mountain, but over the years I have made myself do it when opportunities arise. Several years ago, I chose to speak at Ted's Dad's funeral, a day that was already difficult in so many ways. He died of a rare cancer at the young age of 63. Watching him decline that year was incredibly heartbreaking. The grandkids were all young and probably didn't understand everything that was happening around them. It was hard balancing work and our kids and trying to be there during that difficult time. When he passed, I knew I had to get up and talk at the funeral. I knew that no one else would be able to do it, and I wanted to share those special memories and let everyone know what an incredible Grandpa he was to his 5 young grandchildren. I couldn't help a lot in his care at the end of his life, but I could step up and do my part as we said goodbye. In that moment of sadness, I mustered up enough courage to stand up in front of a packed room of grieving friends and family, speak from my heart and represent our family in a way that felt personal. This was definitely out of character for me, as I am historically not someone that volunteers to get up and speak in front of a crowd of people. But this was one time that I was willing to put my fear aside, do what felt right in my heart, and I have no regrets, except that I maybe should have taken Natalie up there with me. Instead she started crying, providing a distraction and had to be taken out of the room by my Mom.

A few years later, I briefly spoke at my Grandma's funeral as well, another testament of my growth in becoming a less anxious version of myself. What an honor it was to be able to say a few words about a woman who meant so much to me and everyone she encountered. I sure do miss those phone calls, holiday greeting cards, and visits with her, and what I would do to have one more chance to chat about life at her dining room table. What a gift she was to me and all who knew her. She was always so proud of me, offering nothing but love and encouragement as I pursued my dreams. She would have loved to have read this book, as she loved telling stories and would have been so proud to have read mine.

Life is most certainly hard, and we have to do hard things in order to become better and stronger. Our fears and failures are not a measure of our worth, but simply how we learn and grow and do better the next time. God used all of these different experiences to help me grow as a person, and now I am choosing to share them in a way that hopefully encourages others. 1 John 4:4 (NIV) says "The Lord is greater than the giants you face." In reality, my giants were small compared to what others have gone through. They were simply little bumps in the road to becoming the person I was meant to be. But I still had to choose to keep going down that bumpy path, choosing to remain hopeful, not giving up on my dreams.

As I have gotten older, I have gained incredible perspective as I have watched other people overcome devastating and heartbreaking life events and giant obstacles. The fears, failures, insecurities, and disappointments that I have told you about seem minuscule compared to the tragic events, incredible loss, and giant mountains that others have had to climb. I have watched as families have endured the loss of a child, I've wept as we've gotten news of one mass shooting after another, and I remember the events that took place on 9/11 wondering how the survivors would ever be able to pick up the pieces left behind. Life goes on, natural disasters happen, more people are told they have cancer, tragic accidents occur every second of every day, couples continue to struggle with infertility, life happens. Life is hard. The little things like my season of failure and feeling disappointed and discouraged prepare us for big things that require even more faith and endurance. We are stronger for having gone through those little things and are therefore more prepared to take on even bigger challenges.

Life is most certainly going to throw many more giants my way. My time is coming. My world will be knocked upside down, my boat will be rocked, and my faith will be tested. I will get the cancer diagnosis, be on the receiving end of really bad news, and I will face huge scary unimaginable giants. We all will. But I will be ready. I will be grounded in my faith, anchored to my rock, stronger for having gone through some tough things. Having walked through some of these obstacles during this season of life will give me the strength and confidence I need to tackle them head on. It is often in our lowest times, our times of pain and suffering, sadness and grief that our faith grows the strongest. How we choose to react to life's biggest challenges is the difference between finding joy in our sorrow or only seeing pain, anger, bitterness, and brokenness. God is bigger and better than anything life decides to throw my way.

CHAPTER 12:

BUILDING A LIFE TOGETHER

"The greatest marriages are built on teamwork....a
mutual respect, a healthy dose of admiration and a never-
ending portion of love and grace." Fawn Weaver

In the midst of my tough season of career uncertainty and feeling like
a failure, I thankfully had great certainty and confidence in my future
as Mrs. Ted Smith. It was truly a blessing that I had something good
to look forward to during that difficult year. Planning our wedding
brought me great joy and provided a good distraction for what felt
like chaos in other areas of my life. I planned every little detail from
the music to the hand-made programs and send-off sparkler pouches.
Having that creative outlet really helped me in a time when I felt like
I was struggling to keep my head up.

Our wedding took place during the hottest time of the year on
September 7, 2002. Being a farmer's daughter, I was told that we
couldn't get married during harvest season, so any time after August
was fair game. So, like my older brother (and later my younger
brother), September was the month we chose to have our wedding.

We were married in the church that I grew up in, with all the traditional rituals, scripture readings, organ music, and marriage vows. One of Ted's friends provided special music, including the song by Steven Curtis Chapman, "Parent's Prayer." The chorus "Lord, help us let go of two that they might become one. Just like the Father, Spirit, and Son. Two hearts invisibly bound in love. By a vow that will not be undone," helped set the tone of our marriage as we lit the unity candle. My dress was absolutely perfect, a beautiful soft candlelight strapless gown laced up in the back with a cascading train. My bridesmaids wore my favorite color pink and carried bouquets of pink, purple and yellow roses as our family and friends watched us say "I do." It was a beautiful evening, and we were so blissfully happy to be joined together as one.

Following the ceremony, our wedding reception took place at Crawford Community Center, a familiar place where we had attended dozens of family reunions, wedding receptions, and my Grandparent's anniversary celebrations. It was hardly recognizable that night with the fabric lined walls, twinkling lights, beautiful roses, and lattice boards. There was the usual Bar-b-que meal and traditional kegs of beer, but the bottles of wine along with a fruit and cheese table added a touch of elegance that we were looking for. My Dad thanked everyone for coming and joked about President George W. Bush and first Lady Laura sending their regrets. Crawford was home to their ranch that they often visited during his Presidency, so it seemed appropriate to joke about their lack of attendance at the big party that night. We had a traditional wedding march led by family friends, and we danced to Keith Whitley's 1988 release "When you say nothing at all." I surprised my Dad with a dance to George Strait's "Amarillo by Morning," as we had danced to that song many times over the years. My Dad let my Grandpa cut in during part of the song with me. It was a special moment, as I knew it was probably the very last time I would dance with my Grandpa, and it was. Our wedding reception was an absolute blast. We danced the night away until it was time for us to leave. A hummer limo arrived to take us away, and we ran through sparklers as the rain started to fall. Still in our wedding attire, now wet from the rain, we waved goodbye to our family and friends.

The limo took us back to Belton, and just a few hours later, we were driving down to Houston to leave on a flight to St. Lucia. The excitement of our honeymoon led to poor planning on our part. We had barely slept a wink and had a full day of travel ahead of us. By the time we arrived that night, we were starving and exhausted. But the following days in our tropical paradise were amazing. St. Lucia was an absolutely beautiful island, and we soaked up plenty of sun while enjoying our time together. Ted played some golf, and I happily relaxed by the pool with a book and plenty of cold blended concoctions. The weather was perfect until September 11th, one year following the 9/11 attacks. It appropriately rained all day long, as if the world was mourning. We stayed inside, watching video footage most of the day. It was a gloomy day, and I thought a lot about my Grandpa and wondered how he was doing. It was hard being so far away, worried that he might not be doing well. As sad as it was to leave our relaxing resort in paradise, we were also ready to go home and start our new life together.

Our first year of marriage was spent living in a 2-bedroom apartment in Belton. My Grandparents purchased our new living room furniture for us as a wedding gift, giving us a great start. The rest of the place was furnished with hand-me-down furniture from our family. We looked forward to slowly upgrading our furniture when we eventually moved into a house. Having a dog in an apartment was difficult, and we looked forward to buying a place of our own. We'd often drive around on Sundays looking at houses and dreaming of our first home. After a year of looking, we purchased our first house in the nearby town. It was a great house in a convenient location to both of our jobs, and we actually ended up living there for 10 years. The people we bought it from ended up leaving their huge aquarium filled with interesting fish. It was a fun hobby for several years, but then became a huge chore and took up a lot of space. We breathed a sigh of relief when we sold it and no longer had to worry about the several hours a month it took to maintain it. It was fun making improvements to the house over the years. Every year we came up with a new project, and we did a lot of the work ourselves. When we built and moved to our current home, we actually kept our first house as a rental property, an investment for the girl's college education. Years later, we purchased a 2nd rental property down the road, that way each girl would have their own "college fund." Ted was smart when it came to financial planning and decisions. Adding the landlord "hat" to his many hats didn't come without stress, but overall it was a profitable decision that allowed us to prepare for our girls' future.

As I write this book, we have been happily married for over 17 years. It hasn't been without some heavy seasons, but overall our marriage has been successful for several reasons. Most importantly, our faith and walk with Christ has always been at the foundation of our marriage. We value our commitment to each other and our family, even during tough seasons. On our wedding day, we vowed to love each other in sickness and in health all the days of our lives, and we intend to keep that sacred promise to each other. The sickness thing has already been tested a few times in our marriage, as Ted has been hospitalized and gone through not one, but two major surgeries. Being a nurse during both of those emergency surgeries, along with some complications after one of the surgeries helped me be an even better caregiver for him. He was also a huge help to me during my recovery after having babies. We've taken care of each other even during our weakest and most vulnerable times. But that's what marriage is all about. Marriage isn't just roses and fairytales. Marriage is falling in love over and over again with the same person as we each grow and change over time. It's definitely a journey and requires an intentional investment to keep it strong. Marriage is learning to forgive and extend a never-ending portion of grace, even when we don't feel like the other person deserves it. Marriage is never giving up, committing to building a life together until death parts us.

It's been said that teamwork makes the dream work. And Ted and I definitely make a great team. We have always shared in the day to day, sometimes monotonous chores and tasks that make up our life. After having kids, this partnership became even more important as we navigated our new busier season. As two working parents, we have had to be intentional about making sure we work together to get all the things done. Our days often look like waking up early, getting everyone ready for work and school and leaving the house by 7:15am. We work all day and start arriving home after 5pm, immediately cooking dinner and getting ready for our evening activities. We sometimes have to divide and conquer in order to get people where they need to be. We do homework, watch a little TV to unwind and get ready for bedtime by 9pm. These weekdays are sometimes hectic and tiresome, as Ted will often have meetings or things he has to attend in the evening, throwing a little wrench into our routine. But we take it as it comes, doing the best we can do and asking for help when we need it.

Thankfully I am off on Thursdays, which allow a day for me to get all the cleaning and laundry and errands done, so that weekends can be dedicated to family time, relaxation, church, and getting ready for another week. We have elicited help with the yard, so that Ted doesn't spend hours mowing every weekend. If I didn't have Thursdays off, I would definitely get help in the way of a cleaning lady. I do enjoy cleaning my own house though. Over the years, we have figured out where we are best used when it comes to managing the household. Ted tends to manage all the finances, household repairs, car upkeep, and our rental properties, while I tend to be the one that does the cleaning and laundry and shopping. We often share in the cooking and kitchen duty. This division of tasks has worked well for us for many years.

Our marriage also works, because we love spending time together. During our many years before kids, time together was easily accomplished. Our evenings were spent watching our favorite TV shows, going for a run or going to the gym together, and enjoying date nights at our favorite restaurants. We loved sharing a good bottle of wine and a yummy meal during happy hour, or just going for drives together on a Sunday afternoon. We also enjoyed going on weekend getaways and yearly vacations together alone or with our group of friends. Those 7 years of marriage before kids were incredible years filled with adventure and fun, and I'm so glad we had that time to build our relationship without the added stress of parenting.

Obviously, this has become more and more difficult as we now have 2 kids. We still love spending time together, but we have less time to work with, and we have to be more intentional. Our date nights happen less often, our runs are usually solo runs, our TV shows have been traded for kid shows and movies, and our relaxing getaways have turned into family vacations as we try to visit all 50 states with the girls. Our time together just looks a little different during this season we are currently in. We try our best to carve out time for date nights, we enjoy sitting together watching our girls play their sports, and we look forward to evening walks with our dog. When our weekends afford us the opportunity to have a babysitter in the form of grandparents, we jump on it and enjoy our time together, relaxing and reconnecting at one of our favorite places.

As much as we like spending time together, we have also learned to appreciate the importance of time away from each other. This has been more of a journey for me. The 25-year-old version of me would get her feelings hurt when Ted wanted to go away for a weekend with his guy friends to hunt or fish or do whatever it is that guys do. I hated the thought of being left at home alone for the weekend, while he went off to play. And after having babies, this feeling doubled, as he was not only leaving me, but me alone with 1 or 2 babies for the weekend. I mean, how was I to survive 1 or 2 days alone with our children? It seems so silly to think about it now, but it was truly how I felt during those years. I didn't grow up with parents going away with their girl or guy friends. My parents didn't really have hobbies outside of work and spending time with us, so the value of alone time and time for friendships just wasn't something that was modeled to me. They'd occasionally get away with other couples for a night out or a fun trip, but it was always with other couples. Therefore, when Ted wanted to get away several times a year with his friends, I questioned his commitment to me. It was immature of me to think that just because he wanted to go hunting with his friends for a couple of days, that he was choosing them over me.

Thankfully, I now have a better understanding of the importance of these relationships with our friends and also the value of alone time. I love my alone time. I don't think I could survive without it. With the stressors of work and keeping up the house and raising young kids, I value time to myself to do whatever I want. Whether it is an hour or two away to grab a Starbucks drink and walk around Target without kids or going on a long run with music in my ears or getting away for a girl's night or weekend with by best girlfriends, this time is precious. It's important to connect with other people that are in the same season of life as you, to have fun and share stories with. Since I find value in this time alone and with friends, I owe it to Ted to also have this time as well. We now encourage each other to get away as often as possible. It's good for our marriage, it's important for our sanity, and neither one of us question when the other wants to do something.

Finally, we both want a fun and fulfilling life and share the same passion and drive and hustle it takes to get it. We dream big, set goals, and sometimes make big moves. Most importantly, we never question each other's goals, but simply support them. When Ted set the lofty goal of running his 1st marathon, I encouraged him every step of the way, never questioning his intention or the time he would have to put in to reach his goal. This meant me watching the girls while he went on his long runs, often taking him water and cheering him on from the car. He did the same for me when I trained for mine. When he decided that we needed to purchase another rental property, I trusted his wisdom and supported the decision, even though it made me a little nervous. When he decided to go back to school for his doctorate, I had to pick up the slack for our family in order for him to do this. These last 5-6 years of watching him work on this dream has added stress and sometimes frustration, but I owe it to him to be a supportive wife while he accomplishes this goal. And I know he will support my future dreams as well. I can think of countless ways we have supported each other's goals and dreams in a pursuit of a better life over the years. We both work hard but want to play hard as well. We have never stopped learning or growing and continue to find ways to challenge ourselves. We get one life, once chance and we intend to live life to the fullest while glorifying God in all we do.

The times we have had the most difficulty in our marriage are when we've had strong opinions, and both want to be right. I've learned that I either want to be right or want to be happy and have to decide which is more important. And being happy is definitely more important than being right. We've definitely learned to be less opinionated and more easy-going when it comes to certain issues. It's just not worth saying the thing or having a strong opinion when we know it will lead to someone being unhappy. Other struggles have been when there is poor communication and also when we are not focused on giving each other the right kind of attention. Understanding each other's love language is important, as mine is quite different than his. I like to know that I am seen and heard and appreciated for what I do; I love words of affirmation and encouragement. Ted likes physical touch as a way of feeling loved and respected. We were probably better at this when we were dating or early in our marriage as we were truly pursuing one another. Being married for 17 years sometimes makes you forget that you have to continue dating each other and figuring out each other's love language. We are both great at doing acts of service for each other but could do better in the other areas.

We have also struggled when we are co-dependent on each other for our happiness and the way we take care of ourselves. I have learned that I can't depend on Ted for my own sense of happiness or joy. Nor can I depend on him for motivating me to take care of myself when it comes to my health and habits. Yes, it definitely helps when he is in a great mood and motivated to take care of his health. But during the seasons when he is not as motivated to run or have healthy habits, when he is focused on other things, when he is stressed with work or pursuing his doctorate degree, I can't let all my motivation and healthy habits go to the wayside. I have to pull from my own internal motivation to continue waking up early, going for runs, signing up for my own races, pursuing my own dreams. I have to choose happiness for myself, look for my own joy every day, create my own habits, and stay in my own lane, not letting what he is doing or not doing affect my goals. And the same goes for him. He can't depend on me alone for his sense of joy or motivation. He has to be internally driven to pursue his own goals and dreams, go on his own health journey, and not let what I am doing or not doing affect his motivation to keep going. Each of us will have seasons where we are feeling more or less motivated to pursue different things, but we can't be co-dependent on the other for external motivation or happiness. We have to be okay with that. We have to be okay with doing our own thing, not beating the other person up because they aren't on the same journey or pursuing the same thing. It's taken me a while to realize this, but it is so releasing now that I have come to this understanding. I am in charge of how I feel and how my day goes. I am responsible for my own motivation and internal drive to pursue the things I want to pursue, just as Ted is in charge of his own goals and dreams. Yes, it's nice when we are on the same page, but it's not always going to be like that, and I have to be okay with pursuing something that is important to me even when he is not sharing the same journey.

Our marriage is a gift, and we continue to work on it every day, hoping to model a loving relationship to our girls. They learn by watching, so it's our intention to show them that we are kind and loving to one another, honest with each other, say we are sorry when we make mistakes, and work together in a way that serves our family and honors God. We must pour into our marriage before we can pour into others, and I intend to keep pouring into ours as long as we are on this earth. I am most certain that this verse in Corinthians was read at our wedding as it is often read at most weddings, and it absolutely still stands true today. "Love is patient, love is kind. It does not envy, it does not boast, it is not proud. It does not dishonor others, it is not self-seeking, it is no easily angered, it keeps no record of wrongs." 1 Corinthians 13: 4-5 (NIV)

A long and happy marriage that stands the test of time is a choice. It takes work and commitment to make it great. Learning the importance of good communication, teamwork, supporting each other's goals and dreams, respecting one another and loving each other in a way that pleases God is how marriages stay alive. Making time for each other, dating one another, and continuing to pursue each other is important. The kids we are raising will soon be gone, and the job we spend so much time at will simply be something we used to do, but our spouse is forever. So why wouldn't you want to work on keeping that marriage alive? I pray that God continues to bless our marriage as well as yours.

CHAPTER 13:

BECOMING PARENTS TO OUR GIRLS

*"Children are a gift from the Lord; they are a reward
from Him." Psalms 127:3 (NIV)*

We were married over 5 glorious years before we decided to start a
family. Ted referred to it as the "5-year plan," and looking back, I'm
so glad we waited. Those early years of marriage were spent focusing
on each other, buying our first home and fixing it up, taking yearly
trips with our friends, getting more stable in our careers, and both
completing our master's degrees. Ted didn't end up going to medical
school after all, but instead pursued a career in education and worked
his way up to school administration. Lots of our friends were
starting to have kids, and we decided it was time for us to do the
same. However, our "5-year plan" timing wasn't necessarily God's
timing. It ended up being another season of life that challenged me
as I watched our friends become parents one after another, while I
saw nothing, but negative pregnancy tests each month we tried. It
was discouraging, as I thought the process would be easier. I thought
I'd get pregnant right away. But instead God taught us an important

lesson of patience during our journey to become parents.

After a year of trying to get pregnant on our own with feelings of disappointment each month, we went and saw a fertility doctor. He decided to start me on a medication to help me get pregnant, but after several more months with no success, he got a little bit more aggressive. We did a special procedure that was quite painful and also involved injections, but once again we were saddened to find out that it was not successful. Those familiar feelings of failure that I had held felt years before suddenly returned as I wondered why my body wouldn't do what it was made to do. Even with intervention, I wasn't getting pregnant. But we carried on, not losing hope of becoming parents. The following month, we tried it again; hopeful that it would work this time, and I would see the positive pregnancy test I was praying for. Thankfully our time of waiting was over; I found out I was pregnant. It took 18 long months, but we were finally on our journey to becoming parents. 1 Samuel: 1:27 (NIV) says "For this child I have prayed." God's timing was the right timing. Several months later, the ultrasound revealed that we would be having a daughter, and I was absolutely thrilled. We decided on the name Avery Renee, as my middle name was also Renee and we would have the same initials. I couldn't wait to be a Mom to a little girl. I had dreamed of this day for so long, and my heart was bursting with joy.

Despite the usual morning sickness and fatigue in the first few months, the pregnancy was going well until I was nearly 36 weeks along. I went to work that day and just didn't feel right. I could tell that the baby wasn't moving as much as usual, and it started to worry me. I got home that night and did kick counts while consuming some sugar, and still felt like she wasn't moving enough. I called the hospital and they told me to come in right away. I was monitored for a while and was told that the baby wasn't as active, but still appeared to be okay. However, they scheduled an appointment for me the following day. I went in to see my nurse practitioner on August 12,

2009, and she immediately ordered a non-stress test. I wasn't there for long before they decided to roll me over to labor and delivery. I was met by my doctor who voiced concerns about the baby and the need to go ahead and get her out. She ultimately decided to do an emergency C-section. It was a scary moment, not knowing what was about to happen. We were not prepared to have a baby that day. We didn't even have our camera or bag. We hadn't notified family or made arrangements for our dogs. I was not supposed to have the baby for another 4 weeks. Would she be okay? Would I be okay? So many thoughts went through my head, but there no time for questions or delay. She needed to come out.

We quickly notified my parents before I was rolled into the surgical room and was given a spinal for the surgery. An oxygen mask was placed on my worried face as my body started to go numb. It was a really strange feeling, being numb, but also being awake and aware of the doctor tugging on my body and eventually seeing a tiny 5 lb. 14oz baby being pulled out. Ted was there for the entire thing, nervous for me and our baby. It was amazing and scary all at the same time. When they were done stitching me up and everything appeared well, we were rolled back into a room, where I got to hold and feed Avery for the first time. I remember having the shakes and feeling like I couldn't get warm. My family arrived in time to meet Avery, and my sister in-law Kathy brought along her nice camera and took some beautiful photos. We had a little scare while I was feeding Avery, still not feeling like myself. She started turning blue and didn't appear to be breathing well. Someone ran for help and they came in and gave her a little oxygen and stimulated her, and thankfully she was fine after that. Since she was 1 month premature, she had to be closely monitored with temperature checks and heel pricks. She was such a tiny little blessing, an answer to our prayers. We were finally parents to a precious little girl, and life as we knew it would never be the same.

Our first year as parents was a busy new season filled with sleepless nights, washing bottles and pump parts, and drop-offs and pick-ups at daycare as we juggled both work and parenting. Our mornings and evenings looked much different. But watching Avery grow and learn new things, meeting one milestone after the next was worth every change in our previous routine.

When Avery was nearly 1, we decided that we would try for a 2nd baby right away. We knew how long it took to get Avery, so we were prepared for another long wait, but that wasn't the case this time around. We found out shortly after Avery's 1st birthday that we were expecting again. It came across as quite a shock to our family and friends. We announced it to family with Avery wearing a "Big Sister" shirt, and our friends found out when we showed up to a Halloween Party wearing "Bun in the Oven" costumes. It was fun watching the surprised looks on their faces. I don't think anyone was expecting me to be pregnant again so soon. Weeks later we found out that we were having another girl. I cried when they announced it at our ultrasound, mostly because I grew up wanting a sister, and really hoped that Avery would have one. We would have been thrilled if it was a boy, but I secretly hoped for another girl.

Having them so close together and both being girls made preparation easy. We simply reused all of our baby gear and clothes from the last time. We decided on the name Natalie Faith, her middle name chosen in honor of our faith in God and to remind her that with faith, all things are possible. We couldn't wait for her arrival. We never really found out why Avery had some distress and needed to come out early, but they decided to take extra precautions with Natalie. I had to give myself painful progesterone injections every week. I hoped to be able to avoid another emergency c-section. At 39 weeks we were at a friend's birthday party and I could tell that I wasn't feeling good. I was having more contractions and wondered if I was going into labor. This was all new to me, as I hadn't even gone into labor with Avery. We went out to eat that night, and I couldn't eat much. I was getting more and more uncomfortable. By the time we got home, I was definitely in labor. We called my parents so they could come and watch Avery and the dogs. By the time they arrived, my water had started to break, and my contractions were growing stronger. I went to the hospital and before we could get inside, my water completely broke and I was soaking wet and in a lot of pain. The contractions were coming hard and fast and I was so uncomfortable. The doctor was surprised to find out how far along I already was and ordered an epidural right away. Thank God for epidurals. I was able to finally get comfortable and soon enough it was time to push Natalie out. The doctor prepared me for what she thought might take an hour, but after a few pushes, Natalie was out in the world on June 6, 2011. It all happened so quickly. She was 6lbs 10oz and perfect. My Mom had decided to come up to the hospital. It was the middle of the night, so she was the first one to meet Natalie. My parents brought Avery to the hospital the following morning. She was a bit confused and scared and cried when we tried to take pictures as a family of 4. Later that day, she did better and was able to gently touch her new baby sister. Our new life with 2 daughters less than 2 year apart began right there in the hospital room. A busy, but wonderful season had arrived.

Balancing 2 careers with 2 young girls definitely required us to divide and conquer in order to survive. It absolutely took teamwork in those early years. Ted would often take one girl, and I would have the other as we navigated life with 2 in diapers. He was a great hands-on dad and a huge help during that busy season. Again, there were drop-offs and pick-ups at daycare, but with 2 kids and twice the bill. Evenings were spent cooking dinner, giving baths, doing late night feedings, rocking babies, washing bottles and supplies, and getting ready to do it all over again the next day. We quickly realized we were outgrowing our first house and wanted to be closer to our jobs and a better school district, so we decided to build a house in Belton. Natalie's first year of life was spent designing and building our dream home. Talk about adding one more thing to our already busy life, but it was fun. By the time she turned 1 and then Avery turned 3, we moved into our new house.

As I write this book, we have now been in our home for over 7 years, and we have loved every single year. I'm not sure if this will be our forever home, but we have definitely made lots of incredible memories here. As the girls have gotten older, we can both agree that this season of our life has been the most fun and also so rewarding. Hanging up the diaper bag and exchanging daycare drop offs for school and sports activities has been a happy trade off. We love watching our girls try new things and discover their passions and talents. We enjoy spending time together as a family, whether it's movie night, family walks or bike rides, cooking and baking together, working on Legos, or traveling. When we look back in 10-20 years, I'm sure we will agree that this was the best season of our life.

CHAPTER 14:

CREATING MEMORIES TOGETHER

*"Sometimes you will never know the value of a moment
until it becomes a memory." Dr. Seuss*

Years ago, on one of my many trips to Hobby Lobby, I came across a
metal wall hanging with the quote "Love the life you live, live the life
you love" and thought, wow, I love that. What a great motto to live
by. If we want to love the life we live, we really do have to be
intentional about how we live our lives each day. Loving life is a
choice and creating a life we love and can be proud of is also a
choice. I even have this wall art in one my exam rooms at work,
serving as a constant reminder when I sometimes question my
purpose. My patients often read it and point it out to me, saying how
much they love it too. I'd like to think that it gives them a little
mantra to think about as they leave my exam room. We all need
simple reminders that life is precious, and that loving life is a choice.
Life can sometimes feel hard, filled with busyness and worry, but it
can also be absolutely wonderful if we are focused on the right
things. Faith, family, friends, and creating meaningful memories

together have become my main focus over the years. Pointing our girls to Jesus, modeling hard work as well as kindness, spending time with family and friends, and giving our girls both fun and unique experiences is our mission. Proverbs 22:6 (NIV) says "Train up a child in the way he should go; and when he is old, he will not depart from it." My desire is to raise girls that love Jesus, love life, and are kind, brave, productive members of society. What more can you really ask for?

Each day and every season of our lives is filled with both big and little moments that become memories. My favorite way to preserve memories is through photography. I love pictures and I love taking them, making sure I capture every season and every memory with our girls. Having a phone that now takes pictures has definitely made that easier over the years, as I always have a camera on me. Sometimes I have more photos than I know what to do with, but what a problem to have. I know these photos will always be a blessing, as everyone loves looking back at old pictures. They help us remember things we might forget. When our girls were younger, I would often dress them alike, especially for photo sessions with my fancy camera. Our pictures would often include the girls sitting in the spring bluebonnets, a favorite Texas tradition, and then with all the pumpkins in the fall. Even though it took some effort, it made my heart so happy when I saw the pictures, and we still do this today, although they no longer wear matching outfits. The girls still look forward to walking through the bluebonnets each year and heading to the pumpkin patch to pick out their favorite pumpkins in October while taking some fun photos. Seeing how much the girls have grown and changed year after year has been fun. These traditions are simple but do take time and intentionality. As each year passes in a blink of an eye, we know our time with the girls is limited. We really do have to make each day count, and I'll keep taking these bluebonnet and pumpkin pictures as long as they'll allow me to. I also appreciate beautiful family photos with amazingly talented photographers, so I try to splurge on those every few years.

We've also created wonderful memories and traditions with each holiday during the year, giving us something to look forward. Some of our favorite holiday traditions with our girls have included us attending the UMHB Easter Pageant on campus, hunting Easter eggs with cousins, attending the huge 4th of July parade in our town with more red, white and blue than you can imagine, enjoying our church's Fall festival and trick or treating around our neighborhood on Halloween, running in the Turkey Trot 5K on Thanksgiving morning and then frying a turkey, and enjoying the candle light church service on Christmas Eve with family. When Avery was 3 and Natalie was 1, Allie the Elf made her debut appearance at our house after Thanksgiving, bringing little gifts to the girls leading up to Christmas. She has returned each year since then, usually bringing new Christmas PJ's to get the girls excited about the season. Sometimes she gets into mischief, but mostly just adds some fun and excitement for the girls. We have also started a tradition of doing an Advent Calendar leading up to Christmas. Baking homemade cinnamon rolls as well as decorating sugar cookies for Christmas is also a favorite tradition during the holiday season. The girls often wear cute little aprons and we give the goodies out as special treats. Christmas is one of our favorite holidays.

I love traditions, old and new. They help shape our childhood and give us memories to reflect on when we are older. It's fun to continue traditions generation after generation, but also exciting to start our own new traditions. When I was little, I remember making an Easter nest out of rocks, grass and wildflowers for the Easter bunny to come visit our house. Halloween often included homemade costumes and trick or treating down 6th street in town where one house always served up homemade caramel or candy apples each year. They were often still warm and so delicious. We always came back to our house with my Grandparents after church on Christmas Eve to fry German sausage for dinner. We were often allowed to open one gift before going to bed. On Christmas morning we'd open the rest of the gifts and we always looked forward to looking through our stockings. Christmas night was spent at my Grandparents house with my cousins, and always included a musical or theatrical performance, listening to the story of the birth of Jesus, and tons of food and chaos with 10 grandchildren. As a child, I remember looking forward to each holiday during the year, especially Easter, Halloween, Thanksgiving, and Christmas. Those holidays defined the different seasons of the year, filled with family and tradition.

Speaking of seasons, hunting season is a pretty big deal in our house, as Ted has become quite the hunter over the years. Yes, my city boy turned into a hunter during our dating years, and his love for hunting has done nothing but grow as we've been married. The girls and I know that the first weekend in September is dedicated to opening weekend of dove season, one of Ted's most favorite days of the year. As the girls have gotten older, they even get to partake in this weekend of shooting dove out of the Texas sky. Both girls have gotten to shoot a gun and help their Dad bring in dove from the field. The first weekend in October is the opening to bow season, the kickoff to deer hunting. And the first weekend in November is dedicated to opening weekend of deer rifle season. Ted has never been a huge morning person, but he makes an exception during deer season, as he can often be found bundled up in a deer stand with his coffee on a cool Saturday morning well before the sun comes up. He usually shoots several deer each year and has learned to process them himself. The girls have watched and often helped make jerky or sausage with their Dad. We have sat in the deer stand together as a family, went on drives through the deer lease together, and even camped at the lease with friends. Talk about an interesting experience without running water or a bathroom at the lease. But the campfire, s'mores, and stories are usually worth the adventure.

In addition to hunting, the fall months are spent attending all the local UMHB football games, cheering on our favorite CRU. The girls dress up in their purple and gold and we make an afternoon or evening out of it, enjoying the fun atmosphere at the stadium, snacking on nachos and cheering on our winning team. It's become one of our favorite things to do as a family each year. The girls love being a part of the Homecoming festivities and have gotten to experience National Championship victories and be a part of all the excitement. It's been fun being so close to UMHB's campus, staying active in the Alumni Association and showing our girls what it's like to be a Crusader. It's quite possible that one day they will also go to UMHB. We've done our best to brain wash them, and they really don't know any other university exists.

Going to the beach has also been a huge tradition for us since Avery was a baby. For the last 10 summers, we have loaded up the car and drove to the beach with our "LTD – living the dream" friends and all our kids. We've often gone to Port Aransas, a favorite Texas beach, all piling into one big house, which has definitely grown over the years. When we started doing this, most of us only had 1 small child, but the size of our group has continued to grow year after year as we have added more kids. Having 19 people under one roof is often chaotic, but also loads of fun, and we look forward to it every year. It's all about creating memories with our friends. There's nothing that brings you closer than walks on the beach, sharing conversations over wine at night, or making breakfast and enjoying coffee in your PJ's. Our kids will definitely remember growing up at the beach, playing in the sand, hunting for shells and having shrimp boils with friends. The beach is undeniably one of my happiest places. It's truly a piece of Heaven brought down to Earth for us to enjoy and draw closer to God.

Traveling has definitely become a huge part of our lives. We love to travel and plan our yearly trips as a family. We are blessed to be able to travel a lot since my job allows me to attend out of state continuing education conferences. Ted has also gotten to attend some out of state conferences for work or school. We often turn our work trips into family vacations, giving our girls the chance to see another state. Ted and I didn't grow up traveling a lot, so seeing the country and giving the girls a more worldly view has become quite important to us. Almost all of Ted's family lives out of state and his sister and her family are active military, often moving every 2-3 years, sometimes internationally. That has given us another opportunity to travel, as we want to visit them as much as possible. When Natalie came along, Ted decided to make it our mission to travel to all 50 states with our girls before they left home. His rule was that we had to stay at least 1 night in the state, exploring and eating meals at the local café or restaurants to be able to count it.

By making this commitment, we have challenged ourselves to pick states we have never been to, save up airline miles for flights, and take our kids on trips that are sometimes challenging, but worth the memories. Instead of taking lavish vacations alone, we often choose to take our girls, and experience a new state together. We've taken our young kids to places like Las Vegas, Washington DC, Yellowstone, and even Napa Valley. They've seen the horse races in Arkansas. We've taken the train up Pike's Peak. We've walked the streets of New Orleans's, not exactly a place for kids. Of course, we've also gone on very kid friendly trips like Disney World and the beach, as well as New Mexico for skiing. We love exploring new places, finding the best local coffee shop or lunch café and taking in all the city has to offer. Our girls are little travelers; they love flying and know that a great big world exists outside the state of Texas. As I write this, we have been to 17 states together, all marked with thumbtacks on our map of the USA. Traveling together as a family is most certainly time and money well spent. Experiences are far more valuable than any gift we can give our children, and we look forward to more experiences. I'm not sure if we'll make it to all 50 states before the girls leave home, but we will give it our best shot.

Exposing our girls to history, culture and art has also become more important to us as they've gotten a little older. Like travel, I didn't grow up experiencing life in this way, and maybe times have just changed a lot since I was a kid. Ted and I have enjoyed visiting museums and memorials, national parks and landmarks with our girls, especially during our travels. This past year they also experienced their first 2 concerts, the Nutcracker Ballet, and even the Broadway Musical Hamilton. We were pleasantly surprised when the girls absolutely loved it. There will definitely be more musicals and live performances in our future.

Ted and I really try to be intentional in the way we spend time with the girls, creating unique memories together that they will hopefully look back on with smiles when they grow older. Sometimes it's the smallest moments that make the biggest impact and result in the best memories. My special time with the girls often involves creating art together, baking cookies or cinnamon rolls, getting pedicures as a special treat, shopping at Target together, or going to the movies. I also enjoy walks or bike rides around the neighborhood, and I especially love doing 5K's together. Sometimes it's the simplest things like eating popcorn and watching a movie at home on a Friday night or playing a board game or putting a puzzle together. Ted likes to take the girls hunting or fishing; they like boat rides and swimming at the lake. He has shown them how to clean and process deer, how to shoot guns, and how to cast a fishing pole. He has coached their soccer teams and helped them learn how to ride a bike. He has flown kites with them at the beach and helped them ride the waves. He has taken his girls to father-daughter dances each year, often bringing them a rose and taking them to dinner. Most of all, he has modeled to the girls the way a man should treat a lady. What a wonderful gift that is.

As the girls have gotten older, our calendars are now filled with nightly activities that keep our family busy. Between soccer, volleyball, gymnastics, piano, and other school events, we often feel like taxi drivers going from one place to the next. As tiring and challenging as it sometimes is, we absolutely love watching our girls do their thing. We've watched Natalie go from barely doing a cartwheel to doing back handsprings, back tucks, and aerials. She is quite the little gymnast now and we look forward to seeing her reach her full potential, but most importantly loving the journey along the way. She is also fun to watch on the soccer fields and is quite the creative artist. She wants to either be a contortionist or actress when she grows up. Avery has discovered a love for volleyball, music and art. She has enjoyed learning to play the piano, and I look forward to seeing what she does in band next year. She loves to draw people, has a heart for animals, and wants to be a nurse when she grows up. The girls have tried lots of activities over the years, but I feel like they're starting to really find their gifts and passions during our current season. It's such as joy to support them and cheer them on.

Psalms 127:3 reads "Children are a gift from the Lord; they are a reward from Him." We love our girls, recognizing the gift they are, and we truly love spending time with them. Each season has been different, filled with both milestones and new adventures as a family of 4. Our annual traditions, special activities with the girls, as well as our travels will be the unique memories that we treasure for life.

I can't express how important it is to live life with intentionality. The days sometimes feel long, but the years are definitely short. Being intentional with the time you have is how life becomes meaningful and rewarding. Make time for the important stuff. Take the pictures, create the memories. Travel the country, be adventurous, go to the concert, have the picnic, dress up with your kids for Halloween, bake the cookies, build the fort. Make the time. Do the thing. Enjoy each day and every season with your children, as one day we'll all wake up and it will be over. The empty nest comes quickly, and spending quality time with our children is one thing we will never regret.

Allison R. Smith

CHAPTER 15:

LEARNING TO BE BRAVE

"You are braver than you believe, stronger than you
seem, smarter than you think, and loved more than you'll
ever know." A.A. Milne, from the book Winnie the Pooh

Life gives us plenty of things to be afraid of, but where there is fear, there is also a chance to be brave. Bravery is feeling fear, doubt, and insecurity and deciding to do the thing anyways. It's deciding that something is far more important than the difficulty or pain that might be involved. We can't always win, we don't always achieve, but we can always be brave. And no one gives us more strength or courage than our Heavenly Father.

When I think of the greatest example of bravery or courage, I often think of the sacrifice Jesus made for us when He died on the cross in order to save us from our sins. He experienced incredible pain and suffering in His obedience to His Father. His life was full of examples of strength and bravery, but His most impactful act of courage was seen on the cross. 1 Peter 3:18 (NIV) says "For Christ died for sins once and for all, a good man on behalf of sinners, in order to lead you to God. He was put to death physically but made alive spiritually." Jesus was most definitely the bravest human being that has ever lived.

When I picture bravery, I also think of the extraordinary heroic actions of people often wearing uniforms. I picture strong first responders running into burning buildings as everyone else is frantically running out. I think of all the brave people that lost their lives on 9/11 as they ran into the burning twin towers knowing they probably wouldn't make it back out. I recall the heroic actions of Captain Sully successfully landing his aircraft on the Hudson River in 2009, saving all the lives of the people onboard. He relied on his training and skills and acted with courage while the passengers feared for their lives. Being brave is fighting for our country, going into dangerous areas, preparing for battle, sacrificing comfort to protect our freedom. To be brave or have courage is to face danger, fear, or difficulty with mental and moral strength. Brave people step up and step into hard things. They take action. They run in when others run out. They trade comfort for discomfort. I am so incredibly thankful for the brave men and women that serve in all the many admirable ways that protect my family, our city, state, and country. Our military and first responders are definitely fine examples of bravery and courage, as are so many other jobs that require this kind of strength.

But bravery is not just seen in people who wear uniforms. We can see everyday courage all around us. Bravery is present in those battling cancer, especially childhood cancer. Kids aren't supposed to have cancer, but they do, and they fight it with such incredible strength and courage. Bravery is living life to the fullest while also managing a disability or chronic disease that could hold one back if they let it. It's fighting to regain independence after an overwhelming injury or illness. Being brave is continuing an unplanned pregnancy; it's going through one painful and disappointing infertility treatment after another with determination to become parents; it's pursing adoption and all the challenges that it can bring. It's facing your biggest fears. It's tackling your wildest dreams. It's often big things, but it's also little things. For some of us being brave is just having the courage to share our opinions. It's being bold enough to stand up for ourselves. It's starting a new school or a new job. It's moving and starting over in a new and unfamiliar place. It's having the courage to pursue something that's important to you but may require more time and work and possibly asking for help. It's having the strength to stand back up after falling down or failing miserably. It's getting back up time and time again. Bravery is telling your painful story in hopes of helping someone else. It's writing the book of your heart, running the marathon you never thought was possible, getting the degree while juggling a job and being a Mom, or quitting bad habits and replacing them with healthier ones. It's doing hard things. Having courage is being strong enough to leave a bad relationship or fight for a marriage that's worth fighting for. It's having the boldness to share your faith, to tell strangers about Jesus. Being brave is uncomfortable. Having courage is choosing faith over your fear. It's being stronger than your excuses. It's deciding once and for all to choose a life of purpose over a life of comfort and complacency. It's choosing to be transformed. It's taking action when it feels scary. It's trusting God and choosing obedience over apprehension.

But choosing courage is not easy. Sometimes just taking the first step takes a tremendous amount of guts. We have to dig deep inside and choose to start. In her book 100 Days to Brave, Annie F. Downs says, "The moment you take that first step, little seeds of courage begin to sprout in your heart." She's right. Each time we choose to be brave, our confidence grows just a little bit stronger. When I was younger, all those times I chose to do hard things, like singing in front of my church, playing the piano at my brother's graduation, and delivering my valedictorian address; those things took courage as I pushed through my fears. Choosing to get back up and try again and again after failing my board exam was an example of being brave, as I refused to let the disappointment and embarrassment define me or impede my pursuit in becoming a nurse. Having the courage to ask the dean of nursing to reconsider my application to nurse practitioner school when I could have just accepted it as defeat was another example of bravery. Going through painful infertility treatments was an example of being brave. Ted deciding to scratch his dreams of becoming a doctor and go into teaching with absolutely no student teaching preparation was brave. His applying and interviewing for numerous principal jobs, being told no many times before finally being told yes took bravery. His decision to pursue his doctorate degree during an extremely busy and emotionally heavy season of our life required courage. Enduring incredible pain while running our marathons, determined to finish the race we started required an incredible amount of faith and courage. I can think of countless ways we have overcome fear, pain, and disappointment over the years, showing everyday courage and bravery in our ability to push through the difficulty of a situation. In doing so, we have experienced personal growth and transformation.

Aly Aubrey says, "in order to bloom, you must grow." Ted and I have both done a lot of growing over the last decade - professionally, spiritually, physically, and emotionally. In the fall of 2013, we learned that Ted's Dad was diagnosed with cancer. It was rare with no specific treatment or cure. We were saddened by the thought of him not being around for his young grandchildren that he absolutely adored. Nonetheless, we all remained hopeful that he still had some good years ahead of him. He started treatment at MD Anderson with a strong will to fight the cancer. He was incredibly brave, despite his endless pain and suffering. For nearly 2 years he courageously fought for more time before going to be with Jesus in August of 2015. Our girls remember spending time with him during his final months, witnessing their Grandpa's journey of courage. He modeled incredible bravery, and in watching him do so, we also learned to be strong and brave.

With marriage, you gain an additional family, and I was lucky to marry into a great one. Like my own parents and grandparents, Ted's parents as well as his grandparents had an appreciation for faith, family, and hard work. Their marriages were built on a strong foundation that stood the test of time. What a wonderful thing to model to kids and grandkids. Ted's Dad and I shared a mutual love for red wine and photography. He was a great listener, and I enjoyed drinking wine with him on the back patio as well as comparing pictures on the computer. He could fix anything and everything, especially when it came to computers. He was an amazing Grandpa to our girls, anxious to help change diapers and feed them baby food. He was warm and friendly, smart and handy, and he sure did love his family. Like my Mom, Ted's Mom also worked in nursing. Her career ended as Ted's Dad began his fight with cancer. Her nursing skills came in handy in those final months. She demonstrated strength and courage as she cared for the love of her life, and she has continued to show amazing strength as she has carried on without him. Her ability to choose joy, find community, and enjoy traveling during this season of life has been a great example for us.

In marriage, I also gained a brother in-law, Sam, as well as a sister in-law Tisha. Ted's sister and I are a lot alike. It's obvious that Ted chose to marry a girl like his sister. We got along from the moment we met, and our relationship has done nothing but grow closer over the years. She has never lived near us, but we have definitely bonded in the last 20 years with each visit, nursing babies together, folding laundry with one another, drinking wine together, running races and sharing our personal growth journey with one another. They have been living the military life for many years, giving me an entirely new appreciation and understanding of that lifestyle. I am so proud of their bravery and courage and service to our country. When we all get a chance to be together, it's fun to catch up. Sam and his family and a lot of Ted's family live in Kansas. I have a fun sister in-law and a nephew from that marriage. And with Tisha, I gained a brother in-law and 2 additional nephews who are definitely growing up with a worldly view.

As his "Pops" was battling cancer, Ted began his doctorate program at Baylor University. Avery was starting Kindergarten, so they both felt like they were starting a new adventure together. It was the beginning of an exciting new season, but it definitely wasn't easy. Ted's parents had just moved to our town to be closer to family, and his Dad was undergoing chemo and other treatments for his cancer. In addition to Ted's busy job as an assistant principal, he would drive back and forth to Baylor sometimes 2 nights a week. School events also kept him out late on weeknights. On those late nights, the girls would often make pallets on our bedroom floor. It was just easier for me, and the girls thought it was fun. This went on for a couple of years while Ted was finishing his coursework.

Meanwhile, Ted's Dad started getting worse, as the cancer spread to other parts of his body. Ted's sister Tisha and family were currently stationed at an air force base in the Netherlands as all this played out. She ended up making multiple trips to see her parents and help out, often flying by herself with 2 young kids. Talk about courage. In fact, she made a surprise trip home in the fall of 2013 right after her youngest was born. Their Dad was early in his diagnosis of cancer and unable to travel at that time due to pain, so Tisha decided to come to him. The boys were both under the age of 2. The trip was filled with all sorts of unexpected challenges, but the look on their Dad's face when he saw them was absolutely priceless. We gathered the family as much as possible during his battle with cancer. 2015 ended up being one of the hardest years of our life, as we juggled young kids, busy jobs, Ted's school, and trying to be supportive and helpful as the cancer got worse. In July, the Smith family gathered in Oklahoma for a special family reunion. Ted's Dad was determined to be there, bringing along an electric scooter to help him get around. The kids enjoyed taking rides around the campsite with him. We proudly sported our "Smith happens" shirts and enjoyed time as a family, knowing the end was near. After returning home, we gathered one more time as a family, as he shared his wishes to go on hospice. We snuck beer into his hospital room one evening per his wishes, and he rose his glass saying how much he loved everyone. A few short weeks later, he passed away at home.

Ted continued to work on his doctorate, and as I write this, he is still finishing his dissertation. He is in his 6th year of working towards this huge goal. It has been 6 long years, as we have supported him as a family. He is hopeful to graduate this year. The girls will be nearly 9 and 11 as he finally becomes Dr. Ted Smith. We are proud of him working so hard during this busy season of life. The girls have witnessed his courage and determination, all his countless hours of work at the computer, while still giving his best to work and family life. In the end, it will be worth it.

The girls were pushed outside of their comfort zone in 2018, as we made the tough decision to change schools. Ted took a principal job outside our town. It was a great opportunity and well-deserved, as he had worked hard to get to this point in his career. But it meant moving our kids to a different school district. It just made the most sense for our family to have the girls at the same school as Ted. It was only a 20-minute drive from our house, and we knew some friends that were already working at and attending this school. It was a smaller school district, but not too small, and we knew the girls would have more opportunities there. But as expected with any type of change, the move was hard on the girls. It took time to make new friends and adjust to a new school and routine. It was hard being the new kids. They missed their old friends and their old school. Lots of tears were shed that first year, and it brought back memories from when my friend Tara moved away. It made me sad for the girls, as I hated to see them struggle through that season of change. But it gave us plenty of opportunities for communication, as we discussed how military kids, likes their cousins, move all the time and have to start over. We talked about how change can be good, how it makes you stronger and forces you to grow. Moving gave them opportunities to be brave as they formed new friendships, tried new things, and over time became more comfortable and confident.

In a world filled with anxiety, fears, insecurities and so much darkness, we need to teach our kids how to be brave, how to be strong and courageous, and most of all how to be confident in who they are. We often compliment others based on their appearance or their accomplishments. We tell little girls they look pretty, and we congratulate our kids when they make all A's or win a game, just setting them up to think their worth is based on looking a certain way or achieving greatness. But they truly are worth so much more than their looks or accomplishments. What we should be complimenting them on is their ability to adapt to change, for having courage to get up on stage and perform, for being brave enough to try something new. Encouraging our kids in this way fosters confidence, something that many of us struggle with. We need to make sure we are inspiring our kids to think creatively, spread kindness, act with courage, and be a shining light in a dark world.

The Bible is filled with scripture instructing us to be strong and courageous. 1 Corinthians 16:13 (NIV) says "Be on your guard; stand firm in the faith; be courageous; be strong." We need to model this to our kids and tell them about our own fears and how God encourages us to be brave. They need to see us being brave in our own lives, having the courage to step out into difficult situations, reach for our dreams, try new things, and overcome fears and failures. If we don't model to our children how to be courageous, how will they ever know that they too can overcome fear and step into a more fulfilling purpose that God has called us to? Young people that are raised to be brave, strong, and confident tend to be this way as they become adults. They tend to lead well and love deeper. They are likely to make a big impact in a world that needs less fear and more Jesus.

I see my girls being brave, having courage to speak and perform in front of their peers, try new things, fly on airplanes, take their flu shots without crying, walk into a room of strangers and meet new friends, and do lots of things that require more confidence and less fear. I am proud to be their Mom and pray that they continue to be strong, brave, confident and kind as they grow into who God made them to be.

CHAPTER 16:

CHOOSING KINDNESS

"Kindness is the language which the deaf can hear and the blind can see." Mark Twain

The world needs more kindness, and followers of Jesus are just the people for the job. Colossians 3:12 (NIV) says "Therefore, as God's chosen people, holy and dearly loved, clothe yourselves with compassion, kindness, humility, gentleness, and patience." When the world sees acts of kindness, hears words of compassion, experiences gentleness and patience, they should see Jesus. They should be curious about this loving Father who created the world, sent his son Jesus to die on the cross for our sins, and guides us through the Holy Spirit, encouraging us to spread kindness and love, comfort and joy.

Every day we have a choice to make in the way we treat other people and God's creation. These choices define our character, our values, and the impact we have on those around us. Practicing the act of kindness can bring happiness to not only the people we impact, but also ourselves. Kind people are generally happier and more fulfilled people. We've all heard the phrase, it's better to give than to receive, and it still holds true. When we spread kindness, we feel joy in return. Just being kind to someone gives us a more positive mindset. A simple smile, wave, or kind gesture can not only change someone else's day, but also make ours equally happy. People want nothing more to be seen and heard, so when we simply acknowledge them and listen to hear, we are choosing to be kind, and that simple act of kindness is often reflected back to us.

I grew up in a family that valued kindness. My parents taught us to be kind, honest, and hard-working above everything else. We were encouraged to be caring, respectful, polite, and grateful. My parents modeled this behavior to us in all areas of their life as well. As a school nurse, my Mom served in a role that allowed her kindness and caring heart to shine through to all the kids she cared for. Kids loved her and the way she made them feel when they had to go see her. As a farmer, my Dad showed us how to care for the land, the equipment and things he worked hard for, and also modeled kindness to the people he did business with. He showed tremendous love and respect to his parents as he farmed the land around them, allowed them to be involved in his growing business, and along with my Mom helped care for them in their final years. My parents showed kindness to everyone they encountered. They donated their time, money, and talents to the church, school, and other places in the community. They visited the sick, provided meals to the grieving, fed the poor, and helped where needed. Their servant hearts were a direct reflection of the Savior. I'm quite sure that I did not fully understand or appreciate all they did for our family and others until writing this book, reflecting back on all the seasons of my life, including my childhood. What a gift my parents were then and still are today. Any caring bone in my body or ounce of kindness in my heart is because of the example I had growing up.

My girls know how much kindness matters to me. They hear me say things like "be kind, choose kindness, are you being kind to your sister, why are you not being kind to your sister" at least a dozen times a day. There is nothing that rattles my nerves more than hearing the girls bickering and saying unkind things to each other. I have to constantly remind them how lucky they are to have each other and that they should treat each other with kindness; I remind them that the way they treat the other is how they want to be treated, so be kind. Sometimes it truly wears me out, as I feel like a broken record. I lose my patience in this area, as I just want the girls to be nice to each other, to lose the competitive nature, to lay aside their differences, to respect each other's things, and to be nice and helpful to one another. Sometimes it feels like a lost cause, it truly does. And other days, I witness them being kind to each other as well as random strangers and finally see the fruit of my labor. My girls will probably grow tired of hearing me say to be kind to each other and be kind to others, but I will continue to say it, as I think it is so important. The way we treat each other is important.

Ted and I try to do a good job of modeling kindness in our home and in the way we treat others. The girls see the way we talk to each other, show affection, and do kind things for one another. They see the way we treat others, the language and tone of voice we use. They see the random little acts of kindness. We explain to them why we do what we do, and that it is important to be kind. We are also kind to ourselves. I try really hard to not talk negatively about myself in front of the girls, or any time really. Body image issues are real, and when girls hear other people, especially their Mom, talking out their body in a negative way, it just fuels negative feelings about their own bodies. I am kind to myself and the body God gave me. I am proud of the ability my body had to carry not 1, but 2 babies. I was able to nurse my babies for their first year of life. My legs have carried me through 2 marathons and a dozen half marathons over the years, and at the age of 40, my legs will carry me another 26.2 miles. When I talk to my girls about this body of mine, I am kind. I don't focus on the extra pounds I'd like to lose, the extra skin I have from carrying 2 babies, the stretch marks or cellulite, or the wrinkles. I focus on all the things I do to take care of my body. I remind the girls to be kind to their own bodies and recognize that everyone is unique and valued for the person they are, and we should choose kindness above all other things.

I have been on the receiving end of kindness in every season of my life. I was blessed to grow up in a home where I felt loved and cared for. Kindness mattered. My parents and grandparents and other people in my life constantly modeled a life filled with kindness. They spoke words of affirmation into my ears, encouraged me in various ways, and always taught me to be kind, polite, and obedient. As I got older, I encountered many other kind people in my life that invested time and their wisdom into helping me grow as a person. I might have given up on my dream of becoming a nurse had it not been for the kind mentors I had in my life. I wouldn't be a nurse practitioner had it not been for the nursing friends I had who didn't take no for an answer, but instead took the time to write kind letters on my behalf, making sure I got into the program I was applying to. I wouldn't have finished my marathons had it not been for the kindness of volunteers and random strangers handing out cold water and cheering me on, or the encouragement of my favorite running partner and husband Ted who made sure I made it to the finish line. I wouldn't be the wife or Mom I am, the nurse practitioner, the friend, the runner, the writer, the person I am today without the people in my life that have been kind to me, that have paved the way before me showing me that choosing kindness is the best way. We've all been impacted by people who have shown kindness and a caring heart when it seemed like no one else did. They were a blessing, and we can be a blessing too.

Tragedy often brings out kindness and compassion like no other time. We've all witnessed the way people come together in times of natural disaster, heartbreaking deaths, and other tragedies. We've seen people rally together, lay down their differences and work to save lives and rebuild communities. We've been witnesses to the power of prayer, watched go fund me accounts raise thousands of dollars for a family going through crisis, and we've seen the kindness of people donating food, services, and their time during disasters. It's amazing to see the incredible acts of kindness in times of great need. This is Jesus, doing his finest work, using His people to shed light in the darkness and bring beauty from the ashes.

But there are also little random acts of kindness taking place all around us every day. Have you ever been in line at Starbucks and the person ahead of you pays for your coffee? I've been on the receiving end of that little act of kindness several times, and it sure does feel good. I've had the opportunity to pay it forward, and it feels even better to be on the giving end. I've also been let into traffic, had someone let me go ahead of them in line at the grocery store, been randomly complimented by a stranger, and I've had my trash dumpster returned to the garage week after week by a kind neighbor. It's little things like this that make a huge impact on our everyday lives. A kind word, a helping hand, and a thoughtful gesture can change the entire trajectory of our day. If you've been on the receiving end of kindness, you know how important it is to pay it forward and spread kindness to those around you.

We are all quietly fighting our own battles, big and small, and one kind word can completely change someone's day. So be the day changer. Be the mood booster. Be the sprinkles on someone else's cupcake. Thank the teacher. Send the card. Pay for the coffee for the person behind you, just for the sake of kindness. Take food to the new mom. Mow your elderly neighbor's yard. Show hospitality to friends and family. Compliment a child's courage or politeness. Teach your children to say please and thank you. Watch someone else's kids so they can go on a much-needed date night. Always send in an RSVP. Call your Grandma. Be the one who brings sunshine to a rainy day, the most positive person in the room, the person everyone can count on to bring the joy.

161

Kindness is often contagious. We learn by watching others. One act of kindness can inspire others who witness the act to pay it forward. It's like the ripple effect that is often created at the coffee shop when one person chooses to buy the person's coffee behind them, and this keeps on and on for hours until one person decides to not pay it forward. Princess Diana said, "Carry out a random act of kindness, with no expectation of reward, safe in the knowledge that one day someone might do the same for you." Be creative. Think of little ways you might be able to make someone else's day. That little note in your child's lunchbox might be exactly what they need to see after a bad grade. They might decide to pass it on to a friend or teacher, creating a ripple effect. The compliment to the cashier on a busy day at the grocery store might be what she needs to hear to get her through the rest of the shift and go home to her family in a better mood; ripple effect. Showing up to that funeral, sending those flowers, cooking that meal, making that phone call, sending that text, spreading kindness will most definitely come back to you when you need it the most.

Loving your neighbor as yourself is found multiple times throughout the Bible. Loving your neighbor is so important to God that He made it a command. Loving your neighbor means acting with kindness and compassion, looking out for their well-being, serving them, speaking words of kindness, sharing in their joys and sorrows, and extending grace and forgiveness. Galatians 5:22 (NIV) says "But the fruit of the Spirit is love, joy, peace, forbearance, kindness, goodness, faithfulness." As we love our neighbors, we become more and more like Jesus. He loved all people, and spreading kindness was His specialty. He desires the same for us. He wants us to be kind to all people, even those who don't look like us, think like us, speak like us, or vote like us. Sometimes loving our neighbor just means listening to them or praying for them. I often have patients come into my clinic and just want to be heard. They are lonely, sad, and depressed, and I am often the listening ear they need. They just want to tell me their story, show me their pictures of their grandchildren, they want someone to listen, and they want to feel valued. These social visits sometimes get me behind but can also be so rewarding. God gave me a listening ear, and sometimes it's the best medicine for someone that needs it.

I read somewhere that we will never change the world by going to church but will change the world by being the church. To love God is to love people, and that means all people. Hate has no place in this world; no place in our neighborhoods, our schools, or the places we visit. Our world has plenty of room for love and kindness. Each act of kindness has the potential to create a ripple effect. One act of kindness can result in dozens more, and so on and so on. We are the church. We are God's people, and kindness still matters.

CHAPTER 17:

OVERCOMING WORKING MOM GUILT

"There's no way to be a perfect mother, but a million ways to be a good one." Jill Churchill

Working mom guilt is real, but most often brought on by society's perception of how a woman should mother her children. The perception that a woman is not able to both work and care for her children and family, and the negative feelings that surround this is what leads to working mom guilt. Dads don't feel this same guilt, and society doesn't create this feeling of guilt or anxiety that working moms feel as they return to work. Wouldn't it be nice if working moms also felt this lack of guilt and anxiety for working out of choice or necessity? I've learned over the last 10 years of being a working mom that women can balance both motherhood as well as a career, and we can do it well. I've witnessed it, and I am doing it. Getting rid of the guilt, being present where I am whether at work or at home and choosing to focus on the positive impact work has on my kids and my family is how I've learned to flourish as a working mom.

When I had each girl, there really wasn't any question about whether or not I would return to work, but when I would return. I was at the beginning of my career as a nurse practitioner when I got pregnant with Avery. I had just been promoted to this new job that I worked so hard for, and I was making good money and had great benefits. We were both at a point in our careers where we were doing well. We were dreaming new dreams and looking towards the future. Ted and I had very little discussion about it. I mean, I would have loved to have been able to quit my job and stay at home with the baby, but I also realized what a sacrifice it would be. The life we wanted just didn't align with only having one income. Financially speaking, it just made the most sense for me to return to work, keeping my salary, health insurance and other benefits. Not to mention, I loved my job and felt confident in my calling and the impact I was making.

I was blessed to be able to stay home for 12 weeks during my maternity leave, treasuring each day with sweet Avery, and then returned to my job at the clinic. Our new life as working parents consisted of daycare drop offs and pickups, brain fog from lack of sleep, and me toting around my breast pump and supplies, trying to squeeze in pump sessions in between seeing patients. We'd get home and wash endless bottles and pump supplies, enjoy some playtime and snuggles with Avery, followed by bath time and rocking. We'd go to bed and wake up at least once or twice in the middle of the night, only to start our day at about 5am and do it all over again. Those early months were hard. The struggle was real. When I was at work, I often wished I was at home in my PJ's holding my new baby. When I was at home, I thought about work and all I still needed to learn. I was still new to my role as a nurse practitioner, still questioning my decision making and skills. The sleep deprivation certainly didn't help. I definitely felt the weight of both new roles in my life, as I navigated being a new mom and health care provider at the same time. That first year was exhausting, and I sometimes felt the working mom guilt that many moms feel. When guilt tried to take over, Ted would quickly remind me of what we would have to give up if I decided to stay home. Giving up my salary and benefits including our health insurance just wasn't worth that decision. So, we carried on, and each month our new routine became a little easier. I started to feel like I was thriving and not just surviving.

Avery finally started sleeping through the night, and I no longer felt so exhausted. I slowly became more confident in my new roles as a nurse practitioner and a mom. As I made it through my first year as a working mom, I proudly hung up my breast pump that I managed to use for an entire year, only to realize it wouldn't be on the shelf for long. After Avery turned one, I found out I was pregnant again. Being pregnant the 2nd time around was much harder, as I was now dealing with morning sickness and all the pregnancy woes while being a working mom with a 1 year old. While pregnant with Natalie, I also transitioned into my new job at a Family Medicine Clinic. It was an added layer of stress as I took on this new role while pregnant and caring for Avery. But I was excited for the new job and the better hours. When Natalie came along, again I was able to take maternity leave, this time for 10 weeks since I didn't have quite as much time saved up. After all, I had just had a baby less than 2 years ago. It was still enough time to enjoy those precious moments with her and get used to juggling 2 babies.

Again, I returned to work, and this time we were dropping off 2 little ones at daycare. With my nursing pump in tote, even more sleep deprived than the first time around, I returned to my role as a working mom. After returning to work with 2 kids now in daycare, the challenges really started. Ear infection after ear infection followed by hand foot and mouth disease, surgery for an abscess on Avery's neck, followed by ear tubes for Natalie, it sometimes felt overwhelming. Each time one of the girls was sick, we had to decide if one of us would stay at home or if we should call my Mom. Thankfully some illnesses came on during the weekend or my day off, so we were able to get them taken care of and then return right back to work and daycare. As the girls got older, thankfully the sickness lessened quite a bit, and now they rarely get sick.

Before kids, I was quite the type-A person. My internal drive pushed me to reach for perfection. There was nothing I loved more than a clean, well-organized home. I loved an empty laundry basket, I ironed stacks of clothes before neatly hanging them in the closet to be worn, my drawers were perfectly organized, and my car was often immaculate. I enjoyed cooking from scratch while watching all the cooking shows on the Food Network. I made time for exercise, and I loved going grocery shopping. My photo albums and scrapbooks were always seamlessly arranged. But this sense of order and balance quickly changed as I became a working mom. During the early season of motherhood, I simply went into survival mode. Yes, my house was still clean and there was still some sense of order, but I also had to let some things go. I learned to prioritize what truly mattered. That perfectly clean, organized home became harder to harder to maintain with babies, not to mention a dog as well. My car became a dumping zone for goldfish and cheerios. I realized it was not the end of the world if the sheets didn't get changed that week or if the kitchen drawers became a disorganized mess from Avery pulling out all the Tupperware. I started taking Ted's clothes to the dry cleaners, as my days of ironing became non-existent. Exercise looked like taking the girls on a walk around the neighborhood. Scrapbooks didn't get done. Simply embracing the chaos and focusing on the big things during that season became my life's mission.

Working mom guilt probably hit me the hardest when the girls started school. I didn't get to go to the boo-hoo breakfast or Bible study after dropping off my kids on the first day of school. I missed things that other moms got to go to. Lots of the activities that go on during the day are designed for moms that stay home or at least have very flexible work schedules. I started feeling guilty for missing school parties and field trips. Yes, I did my best to attend them when I was able to take off work, but I couldn't be present at everything.

Each time I missed something, no matter how small, seeing the sadness on my girls' faces made me feel guilty. It's not that I wasn't active and present at school. I served on the PTA board, attended important performances, and volunteered at as many things as I could. But missing one party sometimes made me feel like the worst mom ever. Not being able to pick up my kids every day after school like some moms get to do made me feel guilty. It's funny how dads don't feel this same guilt that working moms feel. Kids don't make their working dad feel sad or guilty for not being at something. It's different for moms, but it really shouldn't be as over half of moms work outside the home these days. And I'm sure this number will continue to climb in the years to come.

Summer is also a time that has made me feel guilty for working. Summers look quite different for two working parents. As much as we'd love to have weeks of lazy mornings and afternoons at the pool together, activities at the library or 2-hour camps, that's just not what summer looks like for us. We start planning for summer several months in advance, as we make plans for various all-day camps and childcare arrangements. Summer is expensive for working parents, but it's also a time to give them some different experiences. My kids don't get to sleep in, but they do get to go to mind-enriching camps, play with other kids, and go on fun field trips. They spend some days bonding with their grandparents, and usually get to play with their cousins as well. Between the two of us, Ted and I usually take 2-3 weeks off during the summer. One of our weeks is spent at the beach with friends, and the other week is usually spent attending one of my continuing education conferences that we turn into a fun vacation. After all, we have to keep checking off those 50 states. I am blessed to be off on Thursdays, so I definitely use that day as well as our weekends to make meaningful memories with my girls during the summer. On a positive note, each week of summer is something different, and I have yet to hear the words "I'm bored" from my kids, which is a good thing.

A few years ago, I had to consciously decide to just lose the mom guilt. Feeling guilty about working and sometimes missing little things or not being able to spend the entire summer with my girls just wasn't worth my time or energy. I learned to be confident in my God-given role as a working mom, realizing that I could work and still be a good mother to my girls. I stopped using the verbiage, "I have to work," changing it to "I get to work," hopefully modeling to my girls that working is a privilege. It's a gift to be able to do something that contributes to my family and my community. I have a great job, and I make my girls proud. I have shown my girls that there is nothing wrong with working outside the home. In fact, the woman described in Proverbs 31 worked. She is portrayed as a woman that works with eager hands, provides food for her family, uses her earnings and invests it wisely, sets about her work vigorously; her arms strong for her tasks. She makes linen garments and sells them; she watches over the affairs of the household. Her children call her blessed, her husband praises her. (Proverbs 31:10-28, NIV) This woman described as a wife of noble character is who I strive to be.

I love being able to not only care for my girls as well as a lot of the affairs of our household, but also contribute to our family income by working outside the home. My job allows for us to live the lifestyle we want, go on family vacations, have health insurance, and save money for college. While my kids are my greatest joy and will ultimately be my greatest accomplishment, my job is also important as I serve our community as a nurse practitioner. My work has value. When I go to work every day, I am showing my girls that women are just as smart, hardworking, strong, and deserving as their male counterparts. Women bring a unique perspective to the workplace. They have incredible gifts from God that can be used to serve their community. In my case I serve by working in healthcare. Other women serve by educating our kids, being in leadership roles, serving the public, defending our country, caring for animals, creating beautiful things for people to enjoy, and writing and speaking in a way that ministers to others. Can you imagine a world where all of these important jobs were just done by men? We need women in these roles, and I love being a woman that fills this need. I am proud of the work I do, and I can see that my work makes a difference. The girls love going up to my clinic seeing my desk decorated with their pictures and artwork, and my exam rooms with my name outside the doors. They play with my stethoscope and start dreaming of being a nurse or doctor some day. It makes my heart happy. Not once have they ever asked me why I work. They are proud of their working Mom.

The majority of my friends are working moms and having this community of working mom friends has really helped me over the years. Doing life with friends who are in the same season as me, sharing the same struggles and celebrating the same career goals helps encourage me and affirm what I do. Just as important as it is for stay at home moms to have stay at home mom friends, it is equally important for working moms to be friends with other working moms. It's important for us to have other women to relate to. It's important for us to see other working moms doing it well, paving the way for us coming up behind them. It's important for us to encourage each other. I love getting to encourage young women coming up behind me. I have students that worry about what it might look like for them to continue their career after having babies. I am able to be that person that encourages them to continue pursuing their dream career while also being a good mom. I love being a positive example for them, reassuring them that their babies will be taken care of while they are away at work, that they can do both and do both well.

Whether it's out of necessity or simply a choice, being a working mom is common and many of us are thriving in our roles. It can sometimes feel like a balancing act, filled with busyness and tiredness, but it can also be wonderful. The girls have never known anything different, so it is just as normal to them that I go to work just like their Dad goes to his job each day. We do our best to model a healthy balance of work and home life, and definitely make it a point to be at all the important events. We try to stress to the girls that if everything is important, then nothing is important. When I am not able to go on a field trip, I remind the girls that I took time off to spend the entire day with them when they had a student holiday. One on one quality time with my girls is far more important to me than attending a school field trip with a hundred other kids or a noisy school party, but I do try and attend as many as I can. Not always having Mom there is sometimes a good thing though. It helps them grow into independent kids and also gives someone else a chance to be there when possible. On the rare occasion that I have had to work late or work a weekend, or attend a conference alone, it allows for special bonding with Dad. Ted definitely has his own way of showing them a great time. It's good for the girls to have that time with him, as he is often the one that has to work late or work weekends or go away a few nights for training. That time with their Dad while I am away is precious time that they will treasure. I know that the time I had with my Dad, whether it was over biscuits and eggs or on our ride to early morning practice was time well spent. I look back now and wish I had spent more quality time with my Dad.

Whether you choose to be a working mom or a stay at home mom, work outside the home or inside the home, have 1 job or many jobs, I think it's important to fully embrace your calling and own it. If you are a working mom, be proud of that role and commit to being present whether you are at work or at home with the kids and just do the best that you can. Ask for help when you need it, find community for support, and don't feel guilty for taking care of yourself and enjoying some alone time. You can't pour from an empty cup. Fill up to spill out. And if you are a stay at home mom, also be proud of that role and acknowledge what a gift it is to you and your children. Fully embrace your calling and own it and commit to be the best mom you can be. Staying at home with little ones all day is definitely a full-time job and a difficult one. Find community for support and don't feel guilty about taking care of yourself and finding some alone time to regroup. We are all doing a great job and need to support each other in our various roles.

I'm not a perfect mom, but I sure do try every day to be a really good one. Parenting is hard, especially with the added stress of having 2 careers, a house to maintain, and the mental load that moms usually carry. Sometimes it feels like too much. Sometimes it gets the best of me. Sometimes I feel like a failure when my girls say or do something that is embarrassing and reflects poorly on my parenting. I wonder if I am doing a good enough job. I wonder if I am missing something. I wonder if being a working mom makes me less of a mom. I've had seasons where I cry almost every single day. I raise my voice, my nerves get rattled, I put my kids to bed with an iPad because I'm too tired to read books, I forget the spelling test, and I miss the field trip. But I also know how to say I'm sorry and ask for forgiveness when I make mistakes. We all make mistakes. We are all just trying our best. I'm not out to win any best mom award, throw the best "Pinterest worthy" birthday party, or be the PTA president, but to do my best every day to make sure my girls know that they are loved, they are special, and they are worthy of anything they work for. I do my best to cultivate creativity, confidence, courage, and leadership out of my girls. I encourage them to try new things even if they are not initially great at them. I do my best to model courage to them as I do things that are outside my comfort zone, as I pursue new things like writing this book, as I push my endurance level as I run marathons, and as we travel and explore new places.

I always knew I would be a working mom. I enjoy working and serving my community, but I make sure that I am not simply living to work. Instead, I am working to live. My job affords us so many opportunities to live life well. Not only do I enjoy what I do, but it allows us to be able to travel, save money for college, and be generous. We are able to give back to a university that we love, support a missionary, give to our church, and contribute to events that serve our community. My job and my income are just as important as my husband's. We are a team and we make a great one. This is not to say that stay at home moms or homemakers do not have value as well. Staying at home with little ones is definitely a hard job. It requires sacrifice, an immense amount of patience, and a servant heart. I love seeing stay at home moms doing it well, acknowledging the gift it is, fully embracing their calling in life of caring for their children and supporting their working spouse. Their role has value just as working mom's do.

Over the years, I've learned to say no to the wrong things so I can say yes to the right things, the things that are truly important to my family, and the things that bring joy and a sense of harmony to my life. Growing up I said yes to everything, because I didn't want to let anyone down. I felt the need to please everyone. I've learned the hard way that saying yes to everything, especially the wrong things does nothing but create tiredness, overwhelm, and burnout. We create our own chaos, and we have the power to say no. We are in control of how our day goes. Yes, there are things we can't control while at work, but we are in control of the other hours that we are not at work. Our calendars are full, because we put those things there. Our life is fast and frantic, because we chose to make it that way. I've learned that I can do everything, but I can't do everything well when I am saying yes to too many things. It's exhausting trying to be a good mom, keep the house clean and tidy, have a successful career, volunteer at church and school, cook from scratch every night, get the kids to all their activities on time, go on date nights, have friends over, serve on various boards, exercise, wash cars, do yard work, and the list could go on and on. I now take some short cuts with meals, I take clothes to the dry cleaners or avoid clothes that require ironing, we have a yard crew that comes weekly, we use the automatic car wash, and I'm okay with things not being perfect. I have systems and routines in place that keep me sane, and I only say yes to the things that are important. I only serve in areas that I enjoy. I make sure to carve out time for myself to fill my cup before pouring into others. I set boundaries. I only volunteer for things that truly bring me or my family joy.

As Avery was recently watching me work on this book, she looked at me with such pride in her eyes and said, "so you're like going to be a professional author, a nurse practitioner, AND a full-time Mom to us... wow that's so cool." I love it that she referred to me as a "full-time Mom," even though I work outside the home. Just like working dads, moms who work are not part-time parents. Just because we leave to go to work every day while the kids go to daycare or school doesn't mean we aren't full-time moms. I still do all the things that any mom does; my day just looks a little different than a mom that stays at home all day. I have to use every little pocket of time I have and be creative with it. I definitely have to be more intentional, choosing quality over quantity. And I have to acknowledge the help I've had from others. I am eternally grateful for the help I have had with the girls over the years so I can work and know that the girls are safe and taken care of. Our girls went to the same daycare for a total of 9 years, and I made sure those sweet ladies felt appreciated. But I was still Mom, and my girls new it. I am also extremely appreciative of all the teachers my girls have had at both of their schools. I go to work knowing they are in a safe learning environment and spending time with friends. But I am still Mom at the beginning and end of each day. Not once in the last 10 years have my girls ever questioned why I work nor have they treated me like I was a "part-time Mom." They see me having a career as perfectly normal, and they also look forward to having careers of their own someday. They are proud of me and what I do. They don't see me as anything less than their full-time Mom.

I love this quote by Maya Angelou "People will forget what you said, people will forget what you did, but people will never forget how you made them feel." As much as this can be applied to the way we treat all people in our lives, it definitely applies to the way I parent my girls. They will probably not remember all the things I said or the little things I missed, such as a field trip or class party, but they will definitely remember how I made them feel. And that is special and loved. I do this by packing their lunch for school and often including a special note with a word of encouragement or a Bible verse. I pick them up from school as often as I can and ask them all about their day on the way home. I make them their favorite homemade dinners, sometimes even mashed potatoes after a long day of work. We snuggle on the couch with popcorn and a movie at night. We talk, read, and say prayers before bedtime. They get lots of affectionate hugs and kisses, and we hold hands when walking into a building. We celebrate birthdays with all their favorite things. I speak words of affirmation into their little ears, telling them how proud we are and how special they are to us. My girls will always know how much their Mom and Dad love them.

My career has been a big part of my life for the last 17 years, as my job is my home away from home, but being a mom has been my most important and definitely my most rewarding identify. I love my patients, but I love my family even more. After a long day at work, I am so thankful to come home and do my 2nd but most important job as a mom. Loving and serving my family is what life is all about. Creating a warm and inviting home where we can cultivate meaningful memories brings me so much joy. Cooking for my family is a privilege. Teaching my girls about Jesus and how to live a life full of purpose is what life's all about. I pray that we are pointing the girls to Jesus every chance we get. I love what 3 John 1:4 (NIV) says "I have no greater joy than to hear that my children are walking in the truth." I hope that we are encouraging them to build the foundation and values and behaviors needed to have the life they dream of. I hope my girls realize their full potential, never feel guilt for being a working mom, never feel shame for having ambition for pursuing goals and other identities, and understand what truly matters – faith, family, and purpose.

CHAPTER 18:

LEADING BY EXAMPLE

"A leader is one who knows the way, goes the way, and shows the way." John C. Maxwell

I have never considered myself a natural born leader. I mean, a leader is someone with incredible impact and influence, someone who is in charge of a team, right? They are confident, assertive, and more of a risk-taker. They hire and fire and have courageous conversations with the people they lead. Leaders make big decisions and work to cultivate a certain culture and environment in the area that they are leading. Besides my time as a charge nurse, which gave me a little bit of a position of authority at work, I have never led a team, managed a business, or been someone's boss. In fact, the idea is quite frightening to me. I often avoid conflict and confrontation, and I certainly don't speak on stages. That's what leaders do, right? Yes and no. Being a leader is so much more than just being someone's boss or speaking in front of huge crowds of people. A leader is anyone that has influence over someone else. John Quincy Adams says, "If your actions inspire others to dream more, learn more, do more, and become more, you are a leader." This makes us all a leader in some way or another. Being a parent, working in a job that serves others, volunteering, or writing and creating something that influences others makes us a leader. Many of us lead in these ways and don't think of ourselves as a leader, but we do influence others by our example.

As a parent to my girls, I strive to lead by example. First and foremost, I want my girls to be followers of Jesus. I don't just want us to be church goers, but truly live a life that glorifies God. This means my girls need to see me worshiping not just on Sundays, but throughout the week and in everything I do. Kids often model their parents. I am modeling a life that honors God to my girls when I choose to listen to Christian music, pray with them at night and before meals, read my Bible or devotional in the early hours of the morning, and serve the community in various ways. I am leading by example when I show them what it is to be generous with our money, when I volunteer in the church nursery, or when I bring canned goods for the food drive. My words have influence as I choose to speak kindly to others and not use foul language. My social media is used to encourage and inspire and not complain or react to other posts in a negative way. My actions have influence as I choose to act in a way that honors God. My girls are watching and learning as I model a life that is transformed by the Holy Spirit. Psalm 32:8 (NIV) says "I will instruct you and teach you in the way you should go; I will counsel you with my loving eye on you."

I also lead by example in the way I take care of my body. My girls see me living a healthy lifestyle, running and choosing foods that nourish my body. They see me taking care of my mind by reading and learning, growing and reaching for more. They watch me work hard while also being a good mom and pursuing the dreams of my heart. My girls will grow up knowing the importance of taking care of not only their physical health, but also their mental and spiritual health as well. We are often our children's greatest influence, and I hope that I am influencing my girls in a positive way to love God, love life, love learning and growing, and love themselves.

As a health care provider, I am also a leader. Patients come into my office every day looking for answers, wisdom and guidance, treatment and recommendations, or sometimes just reassurance. My listening skills and clinical decision making is important. What I say has tremendous influence. The advice I give, the encouragement and support I offer, as well as my own personal influence makes me a leader. I need to lead by example. When I tell my overweight patients that they need to follow a healthy diet, drink water, and exercise to improve their health, I also need to be following this healthy lifestyle. I need to practice what I preach. Would you take weight loss advice from someone that was morbidly obese? Would you start an exercise regimen after seeing this provider? Would you feel inspired to quit smoking if a health care provider tells you to stop smoking, but you know they are also a smoker? It's important for a health care provider to lead by example. I try to motivate and inspire through my words and my actions. I empathize, but also try and counsel my patients in a way that leads to change.

Lots of jobs have influence. Educators can't expect their students to love reading if their students don't see them reading. They can't encourage good handwriting if they have lousy handwriting themselves. Teachers can't expect students to choose kindness and be helpful if students don't see teachers modeling this behavior to other staff. Coaches can't expect their athletes to have good sportsmanship if they don't also demonstrate this behavior in a game. A pastor can't preach about forgiveness if he hasn't been able to forgive. He can't talk about sin without also exposing his own sinfulness and vulnerabilities. Trust is built when leaders lead by example, when there is transparency and therefore inspiring wisdom. It's the same with almost all professions. We all have some sort of influence over the people we serve. If we desire a certain behavior, we have to practice this behavior ourselves. If we are looking for certain results, we need to show that these results are attainable with the right amount of instruction, hard work, and determination.

I lead by example when I volunteer. The girls and I have been volunteering in the church nursery for the last several years. When I care for these toddlers, I have influence. The way I interact with the children as well as the college and younger students that also volunteer with us is an example of servant leadership. I serve in this role as a way to give back to my church for all the years I was on the receiving end when I dropped my own kids off in the nursery. I have the opportunity to lead young little minds to follow Jesus from a very young age. I also volunteer in other ways where I am seen in a leadership role. I have served on different boards over the years including boards at work as well as my alma mater's alumni board. Serving in these positions has given me a voice in a somewhat quiet way, since you know I don't like being in the spotlight. I love serving behind the scenes, sharing my ideas and being a part of something that serves others. Ted has also volunteered on many different levels. He has been part of the Lion's Club for years and helps put out flags on various holidays during the year. The girls enjoy helping him do this which has been a great opportunity for them to not only gain an appreciation for community service, but an appreciation for our flag and our freedom.

And lastly, my writing has influence. I write to inspire, motivate, and impact lives. There is far too much anger, hate, and darkness in the world. All aspects of the media are flooded with negativity. The world needs more Jesus, a bright light shining in the overwhelming darkness. I want to be one that spreads hope, love, joy and a breath of fresh air. I want to lead by example, inspiring others to follow Jesus, live a healthier lifestyle, and choose positivity and kindness.

We all have opportunities to lead by example. Whether we are a parent, grandparent, serve others through our work; if we have influence on anyone's life, we are a leader. We have value and purpose that can have tremendous impact. We are important role models for someone that is watching. We must be who we say we are. Act how we want others to act. Speak how we wish to be spoken to. Listen as intently as we hope others will listen to us. As we journey through life, we must give others something great to imitate.

CHAPTER 19:

LEARNING TO GROW

"Don't go through life, grow through life." Eric
Butterworth

Growing older is part of life but growing wiser is a choice. It's important to grow and change with each season of life, for every season of life demands a different you. Change is good. Change is how we improve, and if we don't change, we don't grow. Tony Robbins simply puts it like this "If you are not growing, you are dying." I definitely feel that way. As someone who likes to be busy, have purpose and achieve goals, I need to keep evolving and growing. Life is too short as it is. We get one chance, so why not spend our life pursuing growth?

I hate to break it to you, but we are all going to physically die one day, as it's a natural part of life, but some will die sooner. Some will die emotionally, mentally, and spiritually long before physically doing so. Some of us will become stagnant and simply stop learning and growing. We will lose our spark, our drive, our determination. We will stop dreaming and working towards new goals. We will stop serving. We will stop living a life with purpose. We will decide to stay in the same place, with the same people, doing the same thing with no desire to change or grow. We will forget to fill our mind, body, and spirit with good things. We will decide that it is too late to work towards the person we thought we would be. We will give up on hopes and dreams, settling for an easy, but less fulfilled life. We will experience sadness, loneliness, disappointment, boredom, and complacency. But what if we didn't? What would it look like if we decided not to give up on our hopes and dreams? What if we decided to keep learning and growing no matter our age? What if we decided it wasn't too late to get healthy and run a marathon? What if it wasn't too late to learn a new skill or go back to school? What would it look like if we started filling our cup with knowledge, healthy habits, and really good stuff? What if we chose to live a life that focused on glorifying God and serving others? What if we changed our mindset? What would it look like if we changed our life?

I have always been a dreamer and a goal-getter. It goes back to my teenage years of studying and working hard at everything I did. I loved being busy, having goals and aspirations, and achieving things I worked hard for. Yes, it felt a little overwhelming at times as I juggled lots of different things, but I sort of thrived on it as well. When I wasn't busy and didn't have a full schedule, I felt a little bored and purposeless. In college I also had this same drive to do well but started to experience feelings of failure and disappointment like I had never felt before. I learned that failure is also a part of personal growth. I worked hard, but sometimes failed harder. It was a frustrating time in my life as I had to work harder than I had ever worked before. I had to decide to keep going even when I wanted to quit. I continued to experience failure and disappointment for many years following college, as I struggled with passing my board exam, not getting into my master's program on the first try, and then my longer than expected journey with trying to get pregnant. Those years were tough. That season challenged me in ways I had never been challenged before. But I continued to learn and grow, become stronger and wiser and definitely more confident over time. God showed me that He was better than my little bumps in the road, and He made me realize that I was stronger for having gone through them. Yes, they truly were just little bumps in my path to becoming who I was made to be. I finally passed my board exam, I got into my master's program with a little persistence, and I ended up pregnant after just 18 months of waiting.

Some people wait years and years to have a baby and some never get their prayer answered. Some women experience absolutely heartbreaking loss with one miscarriage after another. Some lose their child much sooner than they should. That's the thing about life. Life is full of twists and turns and unexpected challenges and incredible loss. We think we are the only ones going through difficult things, but we all experience our own battles, big and small. Sometimes it takes perspective to be able to see that what we are going through is not actually that bad. I have definitely gained perspective in these 40 years that I have journeyed through life. The difficult seasons of disappointment and failure that I have experienced helped me grow into a bigger person, but the challenges I have seen others walk through have grown my faith the most. God definitely grows us in dark places, whether our own or those around us.

Years after those challenges I experienced, I felt like I had grown as a person, worked hard to get to where I was, and looked forward to the next season of my life. I was in a good place, like I had finally reached my destination. I was happily married with not 1 but 2 daughters and had the career I dreamed of. We had established a great group of friends, we loved our church, we were building a new house and life just felt good. I went into autopilot for a few years, working and being a Mom, taking care of the house and our little family. But I started to feel like something was missing. I needed a new dream, a new goal, something to work towards. I started to feel a little bored, uninspired, and unfulfilled. I felt empty even though on the outside it looked like my life was pretty full. I was so used to growing that even though I was in a great place, I felt like I was sort of dying inside. I missed the journey of working towards something. I missed the challenge of achieving something that took hard work and determination. In a way, I even missed failing at something, because in failing I had grown so much.

That's when we started running. Ted initially came up with the goal to run a marathon, but I quickly decided to start dreaming that big dream as well. It was a time in my life that I needed a new goal. I needed something to work for. And training for our races was just the thing that started to refuel me. It gave me that spark I was missing. After finishing our first half marathon, I knew I wanted to keep running. It gave me a feeling I hadn't felt in a while. That feeling of achievement was like gold. Of course, I encountered some bumps in the road to running a marathon, as I struggled with my foot injury for nearly 2 years. It definitely slowed me down, but never halted my journey to achieving my goal. It just made me want it more. I kept going, and eventually ran the 26.2 miles I set out to do. And I ended up doing it not once, but twice, and I'm getting ready to do it a 3rd time, because I'm a crazy endurance runner that likes a challenge. During my running journey, I learned that I am a person who thrives on goals. Goals give me spark. Goals, no matter how small or audacious give me purpose and keep my fire burning inside. I need to dream new dreams and reach for new heights. I am not made to stay in one place, but to keep growing. Personal growth is a life-long journey, not a destination. We need to push ourselves to grow in all areas of our life – physically, mentally, emotionally, spiritually, professionally, and personally if we want to experience a life well-lived. And failing along the way is just part of that journey. Through failure, we grow even stronger.

A few years ago, I started having that feeling of stagnancy again. I had run 2 marathons, accomplishing that big goal despite a foot injury that could have stopped me from pursuing it. I had grown through the journey, but in achieving the goal, it left me craving something new again. Ted had started his doctorate degree, so I was watching him plug away at the computer day after day, working on his dream and his goals. His schoolwork distracted him from running, resulting in less races together. I kept running, but it wasn't as fulfilling as it had been before, as I missed my running partner. I missed having someone to share the journey with. It also didn't feel as rewarding anymore, as I had already accomplished my biggest goal of running a marathon. I started feeling like I needed a new goal, but I wasn't sure what it was. I needed some inspiration and direction to get me started.

In a season where I was feeling a little down, overwhelmed by some of life's unfortunate events including the death of Ted's Dad, I started turning to reading again. I had gotten away from reading books for several years, as I was focused on work, being a Mom, and putting in all those miles. I started reading books, mostly on personal growth, and realized how much I had missed it. It was during this time that I discovered audiobooks and podcasts as well. What a game changer that was, as I was now able to read and grow my mind while multitasking. I started listening to inspiring authors and podcasters, refueling my brain with words of encouragement while cleaning the house, walking the dog, going on a run, or driving in my car. It was just what I needed during a tough season in my life where I looked like I had it all together, but sometimes felt like I was drowning inside. I started journaling and challenging myself to new dreams and goals. I attended a personal growth conference, not like the medical conferences I attend for work, but a conference to inspire me to dream and reach for the best version of myself.

I decided to start writing, which I had always enjoyed, but never really pursued. As I strung words and sentences together, I heard God whispering to me to keep writing. It was as if He was telling me that this would be the next chapter of my life. God was revealing to me that my last 10-20 years were all about growing, and my next season of life would be all about impact. What started off as a little bit of a memoir and gift for my girls turned into an entire book, the one that you are reading. I have many more books in my heart that I hope to write next. I'll have to see where God leads me on this journey.

While writing this book, I also started training for another marathon to commemorate my 40th birthday. What better way to celebrate a 40th birthday than publishing your first book and running a marathon? Yes, I am a little crazy, but we are all capable of doing hard things. And these really aren't even hard things, but just personal goals that require time and effort, endurance and unwavering determination. We are all full of gifts and talents, hopes and dreams, visions and aspirations. God puts these things in our hearts and our minds for a reason, and we need to pursue them.

We are made to grow. Every day we have on this Earth is a new opportunity to change our life and be the person God made us to be. Life is a journey where we try and fail, learn and grow, dream new dreams, and be transformed. We must take responsibility and change what we don't like about our lives and take the steps needed to be the person we wish to be. We can't change others, but we can definitely change ourselves. We can't change our circumstances, but we can change how we react or respond. We can't change our past, but we can change our future. The most important thing we can change is our mindset. Changing our thoughts can change our life. A growth mindset and a positive attitude can literally change our lives. In her book Mindset, Carol Dweck says that "It is not always people who start out the smartest who end up the smartest." What a true statement that is. The smartest people don't necessarily stay the smartest if they choose to quit learning and growing. We are made for so much more. More learning, more trying and failing, more dreaming, and more growing. In some situations, less is more, but in the area of personal growth, more is most certainly more.

In my job, I see so many people not reaching for more. I see people choosing the same thing over and over and over again; the same bad choices, the same lack of motivation to change, the same job they hate, the same poor attitude and effort, the same disappointment, the same results. I see stagnancy, complacency, and also frustration. I hear people complain about their weight, their pain and fatigue, their relationships, and how horrible it is to grow older. It's hard some weeks listening to complaints day after day, especially the complaints that aren't an "easy fix." We all want the quick fix, don't we? We want to be happier, healthier, wealthier, and just more fulfilled. And we don't always want to do the hard work it takes to achieve those things. What we sometimes forget is that life is a privilege denied to many. Each day we wake up and have another day on this Earth is a gift. We have this one life, this one chance to take care of our minds and our bodies, create a life of purpose and fulfillment, serve God and serve others. It we are lucky, most of us get about 80 years on this Earth to make a difference. How we choose to spend our time is the difference between a life of purpose and fulfillment and a life of disappointment. Life is full of choices, and we are the sum of our choices and sometimes the consequences of them.

We all have purpose and can have meaningful impact on the world around us if we choose well. We all have the ability to improve our quality of life. We have the opportunity to change and grow and find joy all around us. Life is worth living. Life is worth fighting for. We are what we focus on, so focus on the good life. Focus on what matters. Focus on what you can change and not on the things that are out of your control. We can be better, do better, and share better each day we wake up.

The Bible offers many insights into our purpose on Earth and living a meaningful life. Job 42:2 (NIV) says "I know that you can do all things; no purpose of yours can be thwarted." Proverbs 20:5 (NIV) says "The purposes of a person's heart are deep waters, but one who has insight draws them out." And Ephesians 2:10 (NIV) reads "For we are God's handiwork, created in Christ Jesus to do good works, which God prepared in advance for us to do." How will you choose to spend your days on this side of Heaven? How will you choose to keep learning and growing? How will you take care of your mind, your body, and your heart? How will you work on your marriage and relationships? How will you use your gifts and talents to serve others? Who will you inspire with your words and actions? How will you impact those around you? Will you make a change, or will you find an excuse? What will you choose to focus on? Don't be afraid of change. Don't stop growing. Never stop dreaming. Do better and be better every single day. Spend time in the Word, read the books, exercise your mind and your body, conquer your fears, work towards new goals, inspire those around you, be kind to yourself and others, and don't stop living. Grow so you can bloom and be a blessing to others.

CONCLUSION

God has given us everything we need to transform our heart and transform our lives, to become the healthiest, happiest, most grateful and fulfilled version of ourselves who love Him and love others. We can do hard things. We can be leaders and have tremendous impact in those around us. We can choose kindness and joy no matter our circumstances. But we have some work to do. We have to use what's given to us to create a life we love, a life that glorifies God and serves others. This transformation requires spending time in scripture looking for wisdom and guidance, having desire for change, reading books and growing our minds, putting in the miles, nourishing our body with healthy foods, having a positive mindset, getting proper rest, looking for ways to be kind and grateful, and leading by example.

But being intentional in how you live and doing the work that is required to change your life is not always easy. Choosing action over excuses requires a strong "why." Choosing faith over fear takes courage. Overcoming bad habits and replacing them with better ones requires hard work and determination. It's waking up early and sometimes doing really hard things. It's not blaming others or our past but taking responsibility and deciding to be the best version of ourselves right now. To love the life we live, we have to live the life we love, and this requires not only dreaming big, but doing the work to get there.

As a health care provider, I take care of lots of patients with chronic medical problems that are essentially self-managing problems, meaning the more effort they put into managing the problem, the better outcome we see. For example, the difference between a well-controlled versus a poorly-controlled diabetic is often determined by the compliance of the person with the disease, whether they follow a diabetic diet, exercise, lose the weight, take their medications, and choose to do the work. I have seen patients dramatically change their diet, start training for a 5K, lose weight, read all the books and articles and actually return 3 months later in a non-diabetic state. And I have also followed patients for years that just don't have the motivation or drive to make a single change in their diet or lifestyle. They often forget to take their medication, have no desire to eat a healthy diet or go for a walk, they continue to smoke, and instead we keep adding more and more medication and watching the quality of their life deteriorate over time. It's frustrating as we feel like a broken record at each appointment, trying to motivate them to make changes, and they return with the same poor results. It's a similar situation with many preventable diseases. Same effort equals same results. More effort equals better results. Long lasting change is the result of long-lasting effort. A positive mindset, a willingness to work hard and make changes, asking for help where needed, and having the determination to keep going even when progress is slow is how transformation occurs.

I have also encountered patients that feel like no one is doing anything to help them. They play the blame game. They tell me no one is listening; no one is helping with their pain, no one is treating their anxiety or depression, the pills aren't working, the prayers aren't being heard, and that God is not doing anything to change their situation. A patient recently told me that he had been praying to God for years to make his life better, to get his head right and take away his mental illness. He was angry, saying that God is not answering his prayers; God is not doing a single thing to help him. He was frustrated and discouraged that no one was doing anything to make him better. Meanwhile, he was not taking the medication that had been prescribed, he was not attending the weekly therapy sessions that were recommended, he was not exercising or pursuing hobbies or finding a daily purpose, and he was still self-medicating with too much alcohol. He was letting his anger and frustration get in the way of helping himself. What he had a hard time seeing was that God was providing everything he needed to improve his life, but he was not doing the work to get better. He was making excuses and choosing to blame others instead of using the tools and doing the work to improve his life.

Another patient from a few years ago also felt like no one was doing anything to help her. Unfortunately, she had many health problems and had lost her legs, but instead of choosing to focus on what she still had, she chose to focus on what she didn't have. She also felt the need to blame everyone around her for her circumstances. I will never forget one of the times I saw her and had a student with me. She yelled at me in front of my student for not doing enough to make her situation easier. She brought me to tears as she insisted that I did not care enough and couldn't possibly understand what she was going through. As I tried to explain that I did care and wanted to help, and I tried so hard to sympathize, she snapped back at me saying that I was not doing anything for her. She blamed God, blamed me and everyone around her for her pain and suffering. Instead of choosing to use the tools we were providing, the services that were available to her, and choosing to be grateful for the life she was still able to live and appreciative for the people who were trying to help, she chose the blame game. She chose bitterness over kindness and gratitude. She chose suffering over joy.

Unfortunately, none of us can control our circumstances, but we can absolutely control how we react and how we respond. We can control our attitude and our effort. We can control our thoughts, our words, and our actions. We can choose to be kind, have gratitude, and we can choose to be graceful with ourselves and those who are trying to help. We can choose to look for joy even when it's hard.

God doesn't make our life easy. He doesn't simply take away our suffering, our pain, or our problem. He doesn't pave the way and make our path easy. But He does provide comfort and hope. He provides the tools and the resources. He places people in our lives at just the right time to provide wisdom and help, prayer and support. All my patient with mental illness needed to do to get better was take his medications, attend therapy to figure out how to put the past behind him and look to the future, get daily exercise and pursue a hobby or goal in order to live with purpose, and stop self-medicating and blaming his problems on everyone else. It was that simple, but of course not easy. It's hard making changes. It's hard taking the first step. It's hard to admit that we need help. And taking all the steps we need to get better is hard work. God doesn't promise us an easy, comfortable life without disease, pain, or suffering. In fact, He tells us we will be uncomfortable, and that there will most definitely be suffering. 1 Peter 5:10 (NIV) says "And the God of all grace, who called you to his eternal glory in Christ, after you have suffered a little while, will himself, restore you and make you strong, firm and steadfast." And Revelations 21:4 (NIV) says" And God shall wipe away all tears from their eyes; and there shall be no more death, neither sorrow, nor crying, neither shall there be any more pain; for the former things are passed away." This is the hope we have in God. This is what we can look forward to when our time on Earth has passed and we enter the gates of Heaven. But until then, our work here is not done.

We can make all the excuses in the world, blame our past or people in it, blame God for not listening, and we can say we don't have time or the resources. We can decide to quit after experiencing failure or disappointments, and we can come up with every reason why we shouldn't do what is right. Or we can stop blaming, shaming, and making excuses, we can stop staying stuck and just do the work. We can get back up and keep going. We have no excuse. We don't become who we are made to be by just dreaming about it, but instead we do the work. We don't lose weight by just taking a pill or looking for an easy fix, but we do the work one day at a time, changing our diet and choosing to exercise. We don't have an exceptional marriage by just hoping for it, but we do the work to make it exceptional, and we choose to fall in love with the same person over and over and over again. We don't have the life we want by dreaming about it. We do the work to create it.

When I've run marathons, I have seen every age, size, and differently abled person participate. I've watched the hand-cyclers compete at the beginning of the race. I've run alongside 70-year olds who ended up finishing ahead of me. Age is not an excuse. Disability is not an excuse. And, no I'm not saying everyone has to run a marathon, but we can all do something for our bodies. Every morning I see a group of ladies in my neighborhood wake up at 6am and walk 2-3 miles together. They provide accountability for one another. They do the work. My eighty-something year old neighbor gets up and walks 3 miles every morning, picking up trash along the way, placing newspapers on people's front porches, and putting away trash containers. We have no excuse. We have the time if we choose to use it well. We all have the same 1440 minutes each and every day. It's all about how we choose to spend our time. I've written this book 1 hour at a time, by choosing to wake up at 4:30am. I'm a busy working mom with a list of to-do's, but I still make the time to pour into myself every single day. When it's important enough, when our "why" is big enough, we find the time. When it's not important, we find an excuse. I have seen hard working single moms go back to school while also working to support their family. We have no excuse. I have seen people overcome trauma, tragedy, and a difficult childhood and come out a stronger, happier, more grateful person. We have no excuse. I have gone to conferences and heard inspiring stories from people with incredible disabilities. They refuse to let their disability have power over their lives. We have no excuse. So do the work. Do what it is right. Dream big dreams and go chase them. Use your gifts to serve your family, your community, and the world. Focus on your strengths and be the light that shines bright in a dark world that needs Jesus. As Matthew 5:16 (NIV) says "Let your light shine before others, that they may see your good deeds and glorify your Father in Heaven."

Over the years, I have grown as a result of the work I have put in. I was a simple girl raised in a simple town with hard working people. As a farmer's daughter, I learned to work hard, be kind, dream big, and not give up. While my anxiety, fears, self-doubt, and failures tried to keep me from reaching my full potential, God continued to pursue me, strengthen me, and transform me along my journey. I used the tools He provided, I did the work, I learned to be brave, and pushed myself into places of discomfort. I learned to be grateful for every chapter of my life, push through self-doubt, focus on my strengths and put forth effort to be the very best version of myself. My calling in life is to care for and serve others. I want to leave this Earth having had an impact on those around me. I have learned that I can do this in lots of different ways. I am a mom, wife, daughter, sister, aunt, friend, healthcare provider, writer and so much more. My calling is the same but spills out in many different ways, and I am learning how to pursue them. In her book, 100 days to brave, Annie F. Downs says "I believe that we all have one calling, but it can be expressed in lots of ways. One calling. Multiple expressions. Be brave and explore them."

I would challenge you to continue following your own dreams, pursuing goals, learning and growing, expressing your calling in different ways. Don't let life pass you by. Don't just be a consumer but be a creator. Don't be someone that simply takes but gives.

Don't just receive kindness but spread kindness and love to the people around you. Don't just be someone that scrolls through everyone else's newsfeed, wishing for a better life, but do the work to create the life you are dreaming of. Create your own newsfeed filled with happy pictures, inspiring quotes and content. The world needs you and your ideas and your kindness. You have value. You have special gifts that need to be used. You have a voice that needs to be heard. You have a story that needs to be told. Don't be afraid to share your story and your journey as you never know who might need to hear it. There is tremendous power in sharing our story. Writing my own story has been such a transformational process for me. This year-long journey of reflection on my life and everything I have learned through my experiences has been such a rewarding process. I have found tremendous joy in writing and can't wait to write more.

My pastor always said to never leave this world without sharing your testimony. This is my story, my journey, my testimony, and everything I've learned along the way. I have lived half of my life, and if I am lucky, I still have at least another 40 years to fulfill my purpose. I hope that the rest of my story will be filled with meaningful chapters of love and impact. But as we all know, each day is not guaranteed, so if this is the last day I get, I'm glad I had the opportunity to share these chapters from my heart. I am praying that you will also experience transformation in your own story.

DEAR AVERY AND NATALIE,

It is an honor and an absolute joy to be your Mom. When I was your age, I dreamed of having a sister to journey through life with, so being a Mom to not 1 but 2 girls has been such a fun way for that dream to come true. I never had a sister of my own but having 2 daughters has been the next best thing, or quite possibly an even better thing. Maybe God didn't give me a sister, because He had something even greater in mind, and that is you. I want you to know what a gift you are to me and your Daddy as well as each other. I pray that you girls will not just be sisters, but always be good friends who encourage each other to be a light in this world.

Being a Mom has definitely been my most important job and will be my greatest accomplishment. Each season has brought such wonderful adventures and opportunities for meaningful memories. I have loved watching you both grow into such kind and spirited girls. You both bring such joy and fulfillment to my life and truly make me a better person. You have taught me as much as I have taught you. I have grown and discovered my true purpose as I have watched each of you grow into the girls God made you to be.

You are 10 and 8 as I write this. In just 10 years, our nest that once held 2 baby birds will be empty as both of you will be learning to fly on your own. It saddens me, but also excites me as I look forward to seeing how God uses you both. I want you girls to know that you have unique value and incredible purpose and the world needs your gifts and talents. The world needs your kindness. The world needs you to be exactly who you were made to be. And I want you to know that you are worthy of anything you dream of and work for. I know that you girls will do big things if you have the courage to try. You will no doubt experience fear and failure as you pursue the dreams of your heart but know that in failing you grow stronger and learn to get back up and try again. I hope that in sharing my story of fear and failure and the personal growth journey I have been on, you will also have the courage to step out in fear, grow through your experiences, be transformed and eventually share your own story.

Avery, you are kind and thoughtful and have been my biggest cheerleader as I have stepped out to do big things in life. You have made signs and cheered me on as I've run marathons, and you have been more excited than anyone else about your Mom becoming a writer in addition to a nurse practitioner. You have made me the sweetest pictures celebrating 50 and 60,000 words and have told me that I am already your favorite author. I hope that in watching your Mom have the courage to do big, hard things you will also be inspired to step out of your own fears and accomplish big goals. You have more confidence than I ever had at your age. You are brave and beautiful and show God's love in everything you do. I pray that you always have the courage to just be you. You are enough, and you can do anything.

Natalie, you are bold and free just like the unicorns you adore, shining with confidence and sparkling in your own identity. You were born to be a performer and love showing off all your special gifts. I love your passion and admire your dedication and determination to be better at your skills. Most of all, I am in awe of your ability to be brave and fearless. I wish I had just half of your confidence and excitement for life. I am so proud of you and want you to know that you are always seen and heard and loved more than you know. I pray that you will always have the courage to keep chasing your dreams. You are enough, and you can do anything.

I love you,

Mom

ABOUT THE AUTHOR

Allison Smith is a first-time author, blogger, family nurse practitioner, wife to her college sweetheart Ted, and mother to two precious girls, Avery and Natalie. She resides in Texas with her family and beloved dog, Bella. She enjoys running, reading and writing, traveling with her family, and experiencing life in a meaningful way. Allison hopes that her writing will illustrate to her readers that life is a beautiful journey filled with ups and downs, but also incredible purpose. Her desire is to inspire and motivate others to transform their life by transforming their heart and their mind. She looks forward to showing people how to fill up so they can spill out to those around them. You can follow Allison on Facebook and Instagram under the Profile: Fill up to Spill Out or at filluptospillout.blogspot.com.

Made in the USA
Coppell, TX
03 March 2020